The Essential Teachings

Universal Wisdom for Creating a Great Life.

UNIVERSAL WISDOM FOR HUMANKIND

The Essential Teachings

©Dov Ber Cohen 2024

Contents

Prologue

On October 14th 2018, our second son was born - three months early. At 27 weeks from conception, he weighed just two pounds as he was whisked past me from the operating room in an incubator, straight into a preparation room which I wasn't allowed to enter for the next hour. When I was finally invited in I saw a tiny, fragile being, clearly out of place outside the warmth, protection and comfort of the womb. His lungs weren't developed enough to breathe and his brain wasn't developed enough to tell them to breathe anyway, so he was fitted with an uncomfortable respirator in his mouth; to go along with the feeding tube up his nose and several other wires attached to several machines which were all working together to keep him alive. After three days of just peering at him through the glass we were allowed to actually hold him, and so began the process of growing and nurturing our child in the big wide world that he wasn't quite ready to enter. Three roller-coaster months later we brought him to join his brother and sister in the warm, joyful, loving home we created to raise our children in.

Three weeks after he was released, we were hit with the devastating diagnosis that my father, just 71 years old, had stage four pancreatic cancer. A sweet, intelligent, honest, loving, supportive man, growing up with a father like him (and a mother like her) set me up for life. After a four year battle, which included two years of miraculous health, he passed away on March 28th 2023. For the last six weeks he suffered from total heart block, meaning each heart beat could have been the last. My sister and I left our families and joined my mother at his bedside to spend some time all together again in the same house we'd grown up in until we both left thirty years earlier. Someone at the funeral said that it shows what good kids we are that we were prepared to drop everything to be with him. I replied that it's quite the opposite - it shows what a good father he was that his kids were prepared to drop everything to be with him. They were an indescribably painful yet profoundly beautiful six weeks as we shared life, and death, together as a close, loving, supportive family unit.

It was during that time, unexpectedly having a lot of time on my hands away from my family and work, that I started writing this book, sitting next to my father's bed as life slowly slipped away from him. I thought to myself, what more can I do to honour his life and his death then write a book about living life to the fullest, and inspiring others to do the same, thereby continuing his legacy in the world.

Looking back at the stories of my son and my father, I realised in the most profound way that *we don't get to choose when and how we are born, and, for most people, we don't get to choose when and how we die, but we can, and must, consciously choose what we do in between.*

This book is dedicated in loving memory of my father, who taught us the bottom line and the key to everything - "Just always do the right thing!"

Dad, I'm committed to doing my best to continue making you proud.

Intro:
Awakening to the Journey

Life could be immensely enjoyable and fulfilling. We could experience a life full of vitality, meaningful achievements, a healthy sense of self, good relationships and authentic, consistent happiness. Yet how many people do we know who are really experiencing it that way?

For most people life is pretty challenging, with some good moments scattered here and there. The most common answers to the question "How are you?" seem to be "Getting by, hanging in there, could be worse, can't complain, not too bad, fine (which stands for Feelings Inside Not Expressed)." Surely life could be greater than that!

This is what I was faced with at Manchester University where I 'studied' philosophy.[1] I realised that very few people, no matter what age or background, were particularly happy or empowered. We were all just trying to ride the waves of the challenges life was throwing at us; trying to build a healthy sense of self, going through the pain of difficult relationships, unfulfilling jobs,

---

[1] Studied is in inverted commas seeing there was very little actual studying going on. I spent much more time at dance festivals and clubs than I did in the lecture halls.

messed up values systems, stressful exams and an overall sense of meaninglessness. I'd never learnt any useful life skills. No-one said to me when I was 11 years old "Hey kid. You'll probably face some disappointment in your life - here are some ideas that can help you handle that." I mean, we were doing okay, but I started to feel that there must be much more to life than this.

In my final year of university I'd had enough. I realised something had to change. I stopped all unhealthy habits, didn't miss one lecture, started going to the gym, meditating, doing tai chi, karate and going for long walks in the park to find space and clarity. I started paying attention in class and researching philosophical ideas about the meaning and purpose of life and reading classic books about personal journeys including Siddhartha by Herman Hesse, The Peaceful Warrior by Dan Millman, The Alchemist by Paulo Coelho and The Celestine Prophecy by James Redfield. I started really contemplating life. I suddenly felt full of vitality, focussed on the search for the truth, for the diamonds buried deep down somewhere just out of my reach. A note scribbled on the side of one of my lecture pads from that time reads "My mind is getting too big for my head." It was a different sort of mind expanding experience to the psychedelic ones I was used to. Like a butterfly emerging from

5

a cocoon, I was finally breaking out of my old thought patterns and conditioning and starting to take control of my destiny.

Long story short, after graduating, I spent the next six years living in the Far East - Sri Lanka, India, Jeju Island off the coast of Korea, Nepal, Japan - partaking in ten day silent meditation retreats, yoga courses, fasting, getting a black belt in Taekwondo and a brown belt in Aikido, volunteering in orphanages, hiking in the Himalayas, completing a 1200 kilometre pilgrimage around a Japanese island and generally immersing myself in local philosophies and practices. My journey then took me to Jerusalem where I discovered the deep teachings of Kabbalah.[2] After walking a thousand kilometre trail that runs down the whole length of Israel I decided to make Jerusalem my home and began to teach what I had learnt and experienced on my journey.

One fascinating thing I discovered was that, although there are certainly significant differences, many of the fundamental teachings of all the philosophies, religions and value systems I encountered, as well as all the many self help and spiritual books I was reading, were saying basically the same thing. I saw that there is a universal wisdom that everyone, atheist to priest,

---

[2] You can read about my journey and the lessons I learned in my book "Choose Life: A Unique Guidebook to Self Actualization"

can agree on and that can significantly improve our experience of life.

What is even more exciting is that, although there is definitely no 'quick fix,' it's considerably more simple than most people think. Every one of us can be experiencing life on a much more conscious, meaningful and joyful level. Enjoying a fulfilling life isn't just for a chosen few; it's a real possibility for all of us. For some it will certainly take more work and support than for others; life can be extremely challenging and complex. However, with the right guidance and the right mindset we can all start to move in the right direction. All we need is to learn how.

This book is the culmination of 25 years of study, experience, adventure, research, failures and breakthroughs. The hope is that it will encourage, inspire and transform people to live the greatest life they can.

Let the journey begin.

PART ONE:
Living A Successful Life

The Three Foundations of the Journey

To embark on this journey there are just three things we are
going to need:

a) *Wisdom*: The basic ideas (which you actually intuitively
   know already)

b) *Tools:* Some simple, practical, sustainable, achievable
   practices/exercises to help integrate those ideas and

c) *The Right Attitude:* never give up commitment and
   motivation, flavoured with light-heartedness, self care
   and self compassion. (Never beat yourself up or put
   yourself down).

If this journey becomes a burden, filled with self-judgement,
comparing ourselves to others and pressure, we're never going
to make it. It must be approached with a sense of joyful
adventure. I understand that itself is an attitude that needs to be
learned; and we will. Of course it's not going to be easy; life is
challenging and shifting our way of being is also challenging.
However, when we value something enough we are willing to

put in the effort, and what is there to value more than a happy, meaningful life itself?

The Three Steps of a Successful Life.

The core truths are usually very simple. People overcomplicate things. There are just three steps to living a successful life.

1. Identify the goal. (In order to get to where we are going we need to know where it is).
2. Identify the steps you need to take in order to reach the goal.
3. Do those things (this is the hard part).

It's really as simple as that. You want to be happy? Find out what it takes to be happy and do those things. You want to give up smoking? Find out what it takes to give up smoking and do those things. You want a good vacation? Find out what it takes to have a good vacation and do those things. Simple. Not easy, but not complicated.

We have to clarify what we are living for. A 38 year old came into a class I was giving and I asked him what he was doing with his life. His reply… "I'll just see where life takes me." Sounds pretty cool, but as we said before, looking around us shows us that life isn't taking us anywhere great. Financial issues, self esteem issues, relationship issues, health issues, raising kids….it's not a walk in the park. So I smiled and said to him "What are you - a jellyfish? Look around you, life's not taking you anywhere that great. Don't be a jellyfish, just being washed around in the currents of life. To live a successful life you need to be like a shark, with clear focus on your goal and the determination to reach it." Obviously there is room to 'go with the flow' and see what life brings you. However even this needs to be within a basic framework of what your vision and goal is. We sat down together that day and he started clarifying what he wanted out of life and how to achieve that. Having a clear goal gives a person immense vitality and meaning in life.

So let's start at the beginning.

What is the goal of our life journey?

Defining … 'Successful'

When you hear the words "My son is very successful," what image comes to mind? For most people nowadays, the image is of a well dressed, good looking person with a nice car and house, thanks to his good job i.e Success is generally judged on financial status and materialism.

Yet does being rich really mean you had a successful life? What if the really rich person is terribly cruel or painfully lonely?

Would you still say they had a successful life? I don't believe most people would say so.

Maybe a successful life means reaching your goals; if you reach your goals you are successful. Yet, what if my goal is to stay in bed all day sleeping, eating pizza and watching TV? I reach 90 years old, hardly ever left bed, watched every show on Netflix eight times and weigh 500 lbs from all the pizza. I achieved my goal! Would you say I lived a successful life? I don't believe most people would say so.

How about enjoyment? Does enjoyment define success in life? What if what gives me enjoyment is totally immoral and/or unhealthy? Would you say that person had a successful life? I don't believe many people think so.

So what is it? What defines a successful life? Why are the above people, even though they are rich, reach their goals and enjoy themselves not considered successful?

We obviously need a clearer definition of what makes a successful life.

The truth is, everyone intuitively knows the answer to this question and that's why the examples above were so obvious to you.

We can clarify this by asking 'How do you define success in any area?'

Let's break it down.

How do you define a successful business-person?

To the extent they reach the purpose of the business (making lots of money through their business) they are a successful business person.

A successful sportsperson? *To the extent they reach the purpose of* the sport (being highly skilled, winning trophies and making money) they are a successful sports person.

A successful marriage? *To the extent you reach the purpose of* marriage (to create emotional intimacy, security, friendship, love and respect) you had a successful marriage.

A successful operation? *To the extent you reach the purpose of* the operation (ie to heal the problem) it was a successful operation.

So now it is very clear. Success in any area is defined by *the extent to which you reached the purpose of that thing.*

So how do we define a successful life?

Obviously, *to the extent you reached the purpose of life, you had a successful life.* It's that simple!

So, now the obvious question ….

What *is* the purpose of life?

Ahh. The age old question. One that most people contemplate when they are very stoned at the age of 16 lying in the garden looking up at the starry sky but probably never looked into it any deeper than that.

Before we give the answer (which you already know), we must understand the immense importance of this. Achieving the purpose of life is also the key to authentic happiness, fulfilment, self respect and good relationships. It's the key to EVERYTHING that you really want. Everything you think that wealth, fame and nice things might give you, but actually don't.

So come on then - what is it?

Having studied philosophy at university, lived in Asia for six years, studied many religions, philosophies and value systems, I have seen that basically everyone on earth agrees on what the purpose of life is. Even atheists, who tend not to speak of the purpose of life, seeing as the idea of the purpose suggests an Intentional Creator, agree that there are two things that we should be striving for; two things that should be our top values.

To put it simply, the purpose of life is to:

-   Improve yourself and Improve the world. That's it.

Or in others words;

-   Self Actualisation and Universal Actualisation

- Be good and Do good
- Be moral and Create a moral society
- Growth and Contribution

However you want to say it, the two goals are universally obvious. Yes, there are different opinions on what the full extent of self actualisation looks like and involves. A religious person would say that full self-actualisation involves connecting to the soul and the spiritual reality, the Infinite Conscious; an atheist would not believe in that. A Buddhist monk would say that marriage would get in the way of your goal, a Muslim would tell you it's part of the path to spiritual completion. However, they'd all agree that the fundamental work of a human is to become better people and have a positive impact on the world around them.

In fact, when you read them you probably weren't surprised at all. You maybe even felt a little let down. "I know that already. I didn't need this book!" Yet if we all know it already, why aren't we single mindedly investing in these things? Why do people feel lost and struggle for meaning in their lives? Why are so many people looking for the purpose of their life? Why aren't we necessarily living a consistently and authentically fulfilling and amazing life in line with these top two values? These things clearly lead to happiness, vitality and fulfilment in life.

The answer is that knowing it isn't enough. We have to internalise it, focus on it and (here's the hard part) put in the effort to live according to what we know to be true.

The key is to not only make these your top values, but to actually consciously live in line with them. That's where the work comes in.

Summary so far

So now it's clear. Success means to achieve the purpose and the purpose is to improve yourself and improve the world. Or to put it more simply, to become the greatest person you can be. Never forget how essential this knowledge is; the greater you are and the more positive impact you have, *the more you get everything you really want* - fulfilment, happiness, self esteem, meaning, peace of mind and good relationships. Great people live great lives. It's that simple. The greatest thing about it is that it is available to everyone. It's totally up to you! If you are willing to put in the effort, you can be a great person and live a great life.

So the next step is to define what it actually means to improve yourself. What does it mean to be a great person and how do we actually go about doing that?

DEFINING 'GREATNESS'

So how do we define greatness? You can be a great businessperson but not a great person. You can be a great sportsperson but not a great person. You can have the best car, clothes, body, voice, house in the world but not be a great person. You can be intelligent, funny, well-travelled and not be a great person. From this it is clear that wealth, beauty, talents, intelligence and career don't count towards making you a great person. Don't get me wrong; you can totally have and be all those things and also be great, but those things don't contribute to your greatness (and don't guarantee happiness).[3]

So what makes a person great?

Well, let's do an experiment.

Think of someone you look up to and respect; a mentor or role model. Maybe a teacher, a parent, a friend.

Why do you look up to them? I bet it's not because of their body, job, clothes, money or car. It's because they are kind or loving or understanding or compassionate or disciplined or

---

[3] You can certainly be a great businessperson and a great person, just that the greatness when it comes to 'person' has nothing to do with the business. In fact, if you are missing your kids' birthdays because you are in the office all the time trying to make another million, being rude to your staff, and feeling constantly stressed, the business is stopping you from being a great person. Greatness isn't judged on how much money you made but on the type of person you are.

strong in the face of hardships or caring or friendly or encouraging or hardworking. They were there for you, they overcame challenges, they smile a lot.

You know what you really look up to in other people? Their character traits and values. Being a great person is measured by your person-ality. Not your persona; how you want others to see you, but your personality; who you really are. Greatness is measured on becoming the kindest, most peaceful, loving, conscious, positive, non-judgmental, healthy, compassionate, joyful person you can be and having a positive impact on those around you. It's not about what job you do and what car you have; it's about what type of person you are! It's about your values, personality and character traits and how much you are using them to uplift those around you.

Once again, one of the incredible things about this definition is that EVERYONE can be great and therefore happy and fulfilled. Everyone can improve their character traits and live in line with their values to the best of their ability. It is totally up to us. It doesn't depend on any external factor; not on what others think of us, not on looks, wealth, talent, intelligence, how many countries you've been to, education, upbringing. It's all up to us to commit to working on our character traits and spending time helping others. Imagine consciously working on letting go of anxiety, doubt, fear, anger, arrogance, laziness, jealousy, low self esteem; and tapping into self compassion, love, joy, passion, playfulness, inspiration and meaningfully impacting others. What greater life could you have?!

It's as simple as that (in theory! Practice is much harder).

Hard to Truly Accept

Although we intuitively know what has been shared here makes sense and if followed will certainly lead to fulfilment and happiness in life, it's very hard to truly accept it. Our whole life we've been judged, and judged ourselves, on external measurements of success. Our whole education system and society is set up that way. When someone says to a kid 'What do you want to be when you grow up?' they mean what job do you want. When someone says to a kid 'What do you want to do when you grow up?' they mean what job do you want. You are defined by your career. My kids (hopefully) would say 'I want to be good and I want to do good. (I'll also get a meaningful job to help people and support my family, but that doesn't define me and my life).' So these ideas may actually feel like a cop-out. You may say 'Yeah, I get the ideas, very sweet, but I still want to be very rich and successful.' I'm not saying you can't be rich and beautiful and drive a nice car and be good at sport; you absolutely can. Just know that those things won't actually give you the fulfilment and happiness you are actually seeking. In fact they often take away from it and cause arrogance, greed and anxiety. Do you honestly believe that the richest, most beautiful people are the happiest people in the world? Of course not. How about the most kind, loving people with peace of mind and a healthy sense of self who are invested in helping others? Are they the happiest, most fulfilled people in the world? Of course.

I once coached a businessman whose partner cheated him out of the business and he lost most of his money. He was a broken man. Lots of his 'friends' abandoned him and he had no self worth or direction in life. Having sympathised and validated his emotions (we'll talk about this soon) we started discussing this new definition of success and self worth. We are here to be good and do good, not to be rich. We are judged on and defined by our character traits rather than our financial status; not by our wealth but by what we do with it,[4] by who we are, not what we have. In theory, he completely understood that.

At one point though he said 'You know I could have cheated and it would be me who still had the business and he'd have lost everything. You see, the good guy always loses." I gave him a

---

[4] On average poor people give a higher percentage of their income to charity than rich people do!

second to feel heard and then said "I hear that - unless the game is to be the good guy." A moment of silence. "If the game, the purpose of life, is to be good, then the good guy always wins! He may have lost the business, and it may not feel like it, having been raised with the wrong values, but he actually won the game, because the game is to be honest and do the right thing." When I met him a few months later he was excited to report that things were great; he had a better relationship with his wife who said he was much nicer, happier, less stressed. He was spending more time with his kids, knew who his real friends were, all in all he was much better off than before.

So by all means, invest in career and wealth and having material pleasures, but not to the extent that it is taking away from the real work of life; self development and positively impacting the world around you.

Understanding What Motivates You.

A huge breakthrough in life is to understand why exactly you want everything you want and do everything you do. Travel, party, play sports, paint, play music, meditate, eat pizza, wear those clothes, work, buy things, create a family, drink alcohol, study, date that person, watch that show .. Everything!

There is one motivating factor in all our choices and that is …
Pleasure.

You believe they will bring you pleasure (or at least avoid pain).

We are pleasure seeking machines.

Now, we can break things down into two basic types of pleasure.

- The first is short term, superficial, effortless, intense pleasure. Having a beer and watching the game. Eating pizza. Buying new shoes. Going clubbing. Although there is nothing necessarily wrong with these and they feel good in the moment, they don't actually transform you as a person, often aren't in your control,[5] they don't lead to growth, accomplishment, self respect and actual happiness, and often it's the opposite - you don't feel particularly good, physically or emotionally, after the sensation has worn off (I spent more money than i should have, the extra slice of pizza made me feel sick, I said or did hurtful or embarrassing things when i was drunk…).

- Then we have meaningful, long term, life changing pleasure. What does this involve? What gives us this

---

[5] you can't always get the girl/guy, your team doesn't always win, the weather isn't always nice, you can't always afford the thing you want to buy

higher level of pleasure? You got - growth and contribution! Working on your traits, becoming kind, loving, peaceful, confident, letting go of anxiety, guilt, regret, hatred and judgement and helping others will clearly give you the self respect, accomplishment, personal growth, fulfilment and therefore pleasure and happiness you are really looking for!

Once again, you can also have nice clothes and play tennis and eat ice-cream, just as long as they aren't taking away from your health and personal growth. You can truly have it all!

A Major Key: Living Up to Your Values

So let's ask some clarification questions. (I strongly suggest having a notebook or document on your phone or laptop open whilst you read this book in order to answer the questions and do the exercises. Actually doing the exercises is the key to reaping the full benefit from the book).

What do you do in your free time?

What do you spend your spare money on?

What books do you read?

What podcasts and programs do you watch and listen to?

What is your normal topic of conversation?

What do you think about?

Now ask yourself this …

How much are the things you are valuing (ie spending time, effort and money on), in line with the top values (growth and contribution)?

How many of them are making you a calmer, kinder person?

How many of them are actually taking you towards personal greatness and helping others?

Ask yourself this; What do I value more - being good or looking good?

Hopefully you said 'being good.' Being good is certainly more conducive to attaining happiness than looking good is. So what do you think about more and spend more time and money investing in, trying to be good or trying to look good?

What do you value more - temporary physical pleasure or doing good in the world? Hopefully you said the latter. So now ask yourself what you think about more and spend more time investing in, trying to do good or trying to feel good? There are three reasons for these discrepancies. We invest in these things even though we know they aren't actually going to take us to our goal of authentic happiness and fulfilment because

1) they generally take little or no effort (it's easier to to curl over and go back to sleep then get up and go for a run, it's easier just to eat the cake than to resist it, easier to

drink beer than work on the core reasons for your inhibitions).

2) the pleasure is more immediate (you only really get the pleasure of going for the run once you've broken through the discomfort of getting out of bed).

3) often it is more intense (short term holiday romances are more intense then long term commitment to working on having a healthy marriage, drugs are more intense than mindfulness meditations).

The opposite is true of the higher pleasures. They are immensely deeper, greater, more sustainable, life changing and profound. The issue is they take effort, the results aren't necessarily immediate and they often aren't as intense. So we sell out for the easy, superficial pleasures (and become addicted to them) rather than investing time and effort in the long term real ones. It doesn't work in the end.

A major key to true happiness and real greatness is to clarify for yourself that (although by all means you can do them) social media, nice clothes, funny movies and tasty food may give you some temporary, superficial pleasure, but they'll never give you what you really want - authentic, sustainable happiness and self respect. On the other hand, putting in the effort to improve yourself and the world around you will indeed give you the life you really want.

So what's the practical step?

Just never eat unhealthy food, watch meaningless things, go to the beach, spend time buying clothes you don't really need or go out for a drink with friends ever again.

Ha. Just joking! That would be unreasonable and unsustainable. What you could do though is commit 2% extra of your spare money, free time, podcast listening and thought to things that are meaningful and actually taking you towards your goal. A little more money to charity, a little more time volunteering, a little more self control in what and how much you eat and drink, a little more time reading posts on how to overcome the challenges you are facing, a little more time meditating, a little more exercise. Just small sustainable steps. What may happen is you realise that those things are actually the most pleasurable parts of your day and you'll want to add a little more. Then a little more. Then just a bit more ….. Until you are really living in line with and investing in your top values of growth, health and contribution and receiving the immense benefits that a values driven life brings.

Write one small, manageable change that will bring you more in line with your values that you can commit to right now.

Living a Meaningful Life

We can think of this same idea in terms of meaning. What does it mean to live a meaningful life? Everyone I have spoken to wants to live a meaningful life. A meaningful life is the key to fulfilment and satisfaction in life. So of course, we have to define 'meaningful.' What makes something meaningful?

Is it that I enjoy it? Clearly not. Eating pizza even when you aren't so hungry is enjoyable but it would be hard to call it meaningful.

Is it that I care about it? You could care about winning a card game, that doesn't make it meaningful. So what is it then? What makes something meaningful?

Once again, it's immensely simple. *To the extent something is tapping you into the purpose, it is meaningful.* If it is taking you towards your goal it has meaning. Purpose and meaning come hand in hand.

If you want to win the gold medal in the Olympic games, going out and getting wasted with your friends is not meaningful. It doesn't help you achieve your goal. Eating the right thing and sleeping the right amount and training hard are all meaningful. They are good investments of your time. They will take you towards your goal.

So, when it comes to life, seeing as the purpose of life is to improve yourself and improve the world, something is meaningful to the extent that it helps you achieve in these areas. You can ask yourself "How is this thing making me a better person? How is it helping become kinder, less anxious, more understanding, more peaceful? How is this positively impacting those around me?"

Think of how you spend your day. How much of what you do, speak about, think about, invest time and money in is actually helping you become a better, happier person? Is social media actually making you a happier, kinder person? How much of your time is spent on meaningful activities? For the aspiring Olympic gold medal winner, it is 100%. What, how much and when they eat. How much and when they sleep. What training they do. They avoid things that will take them away from their goal - no fatty foods (even if they taste good), no smoking (even if it feels good), no investing hours on social media (even though you may look good).

Once again, it's very simple. To become great you have to invest in the things that will make you great and avoid the things that won't.

That doesn't mean you can never chill out. Chilling out is an essential part of growth. Have a beer. Watch some sport. Hang out with friends. However it must be done in moderation. Investing too much time, thought, money, emotional energy in things that aren't helping you become kinder and happier is not conducive to greatness and all the benefits it brings.

So we see three levels of meaning.

a) Meaningful: Something is meaningful if it is helping you become a better person and/or impacting others in a positive way. You should invest in these things as much as possible.

b) Meaningless: Something is meaningless if it is neutral. It isn't directly taking you towards your goal, but it's also not taking you away from it. These things are fine to do and can even be meaningful if they are giving you the down time you need in order to reach your goal; however once you invest too much time in them they begin to take away from time that could be spent achieving your goal.

c) Anti-meaning: These are things that are actually taking you away from your goal. Far from making you a kinder person, they are making you more lazy, selfish, judgmental, unhealthy. These things you should avoid as much as possible (even if you really enjoy them in the moment).

You just made a list of things you invest time, emotional energy and money in. If you haven't yet, you can do it now. Now, categorise them into meaningful, meaningless and anti-meaning. Start investing in the right things and you'll get the results you really want.

A Fundamental Principle: If it doesn't work don't do it!

An even simpler way to relate to living up to your values and living a meaningful life is this - If it doesn't work, don't do it!

If you saw someone with a gash in their arm scratching it, you'd think they were completely crazy. Scratching a wound like that not only doesn't help, it makes it worse. There's a basic rule in life - if it doesn't work, don't do it. What does it mean to not work? If it doesn't

- change the situation for the better
- make you feel more positive, calm and healthy
- make you authentically happier, kinder, greater
- help other people

then don't do it.

Now you may be thinking that I'm crazy. Of course you shouldn't do things that don't work! Everyone knows that. Who would do things that don't work?

Well, the truth is we do it all the time.

- You do an exam or have a medical scan one day, the results are coming out seven days later. Do you spend all week worrying about the results? How does that help? It doesn't make you feel good and doesn't affect the results. If it doesn't work, don't do it!
- You're late for work and the bus isn't coming, you're late for an event and you're stuck in traffic. Do you get very frustrated? Well, how does that help? It doesn't make you feel good and it doesn't bring the bus or get the traffic moving. If it doesn't work, don't do it!
- You make a mistake and then beat yourself up for it for a month (What's wrong with me, I'm such an idiot, what do people think of me ....). How does that help? It doesn't help you grow and change or feel good about yourself. If it doesn't work, don't do it.[6]
- You eat some food you really enjoy but it's not healthy and you eat too much and you don't feel physically great afterwards and you don't feel good about yourself for eating it. If it doesn't work, don't do it.

I spoke to a group of middle aged couples about relationships. I told them that in a relationship, if it doesn't work, don't do it.

---

[6] A little bit of remorse does help you grow. If you make mistakes and don't feel any disappointment you won't grow. If you beat yourself up you also won't grow. We need to get the balance.

They looked at me as if I was an idiot. "Who would do something that doesn't work?" Me: "Well, do you ever argue?" Them: "Everyone argues!" Me:"Okay. And how does that help the relationship? Does it create love, respect and emotional intimacy?" Them: "No." Me (with a big grin) "Well, if it doesn't work, don't do it."

Now I know it is easier said than done. How do we not worry and get frustrated and stop beating ourselves up and putting down those we love? Great question. We're going to work on that soon. The first step though is to at least identify and recognise your thought patterns and behaviours that aren't working for you. Once you have done that we can work on mindfulness, self control, positive thinking, gratitude and all the wonderful things that can transform our lives. *Write a list of thoughts and behaviours that you often engage in that don't work.*

These we can work on.

End of Section Test Question

So let's do an end of section test to see if you grasped the ideas. Think about this question:

Michael Jordan - successful life or not? Think before you answer or read the answer...

The truth is, I don't know him well enough to answer the question. I know he certainly had success in life. He achieved his sporting goals, financial goals, fame goals. However when it comes to THE goals - was he a kind, honest, ethical, loving, compassionate human being? How many people did he help (and not just to get credit for it)? I don't know the answer to these questions, but I do know that these are the significant criteria.

Another way to think about it is the conversation Michael will have with God at the end of his life.[7]

"Hey Michael, good to see you here. What did you achieve in your life?"

"I was one of the greatest sportsmen ever to walk the face of the earth."

"Great Michael, but that's not the criteria for getting in." "I created a great clothing line." "Great Michael, but that's not the criteria for getting in."

"I have houses in 5 continents." "Great Michael, but that's not the criteria for getting in." Michael, getting a bit worried "I set up a foundation to support kids from difficult homes to find their calling in life ....!"

"Ah Michael, now you're talking. That counts... in you come."

---

[7] It's fine if you don't believe in God - the example is just to get across the idea.

What makes Michael a great person is not his talent, money or fame, it's how much he used those things to refine his character and positively impact others.

So stage one is complete. We have clarified
a) What true success is (reaching the purpose),
b) What the purpose is (becoming great),
c) What being great is (refined character traits and having a positive impact)
d) What makes something meaningful (it takes you towards the purpose),
e) The immense benefit of living with these values (authentic happiness, self respect, fulfilment, good relationships - everything you really want out of life).
f) The beautiful fact that it's all up to you. You can do it.

So now we just need to know how to practically implement these things.

PART TWO:

Improving Yourself

So let's look more deeply into what it means to improve ourselves. If your friends tell you they are really working on improving themselves - does that mean their tennis backhand? Their wardrobe? Their hairstyle?

Clearly not. If someone wants to marry your daughter you don't care how good they are at tennis or how many Armani suits they have. We said that the key is working on your character traits - strengthening and developing good ones and letting go of negative ones. What do you really want for your daughter (or yourself!)? A guy with great character traits; loving, kind, understanding, fun…

So how do we actually go about doing that?

Character Traits

First we need to understand what exactly a character trait is. A trait is a way of being, a tendency, expressed through your thoughts (which create your feelings), speech and behaviour. If you have a tendency to think certain thoughts and feel certain feelings - envy, impatience, anger, anxiety, love, joy - and do certain things quite habitually and regularly, you have that trait. If you have one envious thought a month, that doesn't make you an envious person. However, if you always struggle with comparing yourself to others and wish you had what they had and feel this strongly, one would say you have the trait of envy. Positive traits create vitality and joy, and when they are expressed in the world, you create healing, happiness and inspiration around you. Negative ones expressed in thought, speech and action ruin your peace of mind, take away from your happiness and create pain and negativity around you.

Now, your traits aren't your fault. You developed from a very early age through nature and nurture. You aren't wrong for having them. However, you also don't have to be a victim to them. You have the opportunity, and responsibility, to let go of negative ones as well as cultivate good ones. This is very important seeing as your happiness depends on it. If you really work through your negative traits and distance yourself from them, and cultivate positive healthy ones, you'd be living life on a whole new level.

Preliminary Attitude to Refining Character Traits

Before we look at some practical methods to work on your traits, I want to reiterate the importance of your attitude to personal growth. It needs to be seen as an opportunity not a burden. Any guilt, pressure or critical self-judgement actually gets in the way of growth.

Secondly you need to believe that although it takes time to change it can be done. Realise that you can actually retrain yourself and change your traits, if not completely, at least you can lessen their intensity and frequency.

The next thing to understand is that your negative traits do not define you. They are things you need to, and can, work on and improve. If you feel like a victim to your traits and feel that there is nothing you can do, of course you can't even get off the mark. If you are walking around feeling resigned to your fate, disempowered, telling yourself that you can't change and there is something wrong with you or blaming others, then you're not giving yourself any chance. With an attitude like that, there is no possibility of growth. Many people identify with their negative character traits. 'I'm a high anxiety person.' 'I'm so impatient.' They tell me they hate themselves and when I ask why they give me a list of bad character traits. So I ask them whether they hate their children because they also have some bad traits. Of course

36

they don't; they try to guide them and help them grow. Understand that this is a challenge you have rather than who you are. Once you dis-identify with it, it becomes much easier to deal with.

So let's talk about practically and consciously working on your traits. It is VERY important to feel good about yourself before working on improving yourself. If you feel down about yourself and then you scrutinise what you need to improve, it's just going to make you feel worse and you'll just get depressed rather than grow. We're going to be speaking a lot about building a healthy sense of self in a later chapter but for now you can start to build a healthy sense of self by focusing on your good character traits, your good values, your achievements in life, kindness you have done for others. You have struggles and make mistakes, but you are basically a decent person. Once you feel generally good about yourself, and that your bad traits don't make you a bad person, you can start working on areas you need to improve.

A Few Key Ways to Work on Refining Character Traits

Whilst you could go to therapy and spend hours talking about your childhood and what caused this character trait, the truth is that it's often not necessary to go there. If someone goes to hospital with a knife wound, they treat the wound. They don't need to find out who did it or where it happened, or what they were wearing. Just treat the issue. Then afterwards, when we regain some health and are feeling better, we can look into causes and work on fixing the situation in the future.

I'd like to suggest three simple, but not easy, methods of retraining your traits.

Create Your State:

This takes some preparation. You have to think of situations that trigger a negative trait in you. A certain person annoys you, seeing certain photos on social media makes you jealous, being stuck in traffic gets you frustrated, the approaching exam makes you anxious. Whatever it is, become aware of your areas of battle, and prepare beforehand. Imagine yourself in that situation - how you feel, how you react, how you are standing and breathing, what you are thinking, hurtful things you may say, the feeling of disappointment afterwards. Now, imagine how you could respond differently. Picture your greatest, calmest self in that situation. How would you be standing and breathing? What would you be thinking, saying, doing? (See yourself sitting in the traffic jam breathing deeply, listening to some uplifting tunes, saying to yourself "even if I'm late, I'm sure it will be okay.") Imagine as vividly as you can being in that situation and responding in the highest way possible. Then imagine the great feeling you'd have if you did this; self respect, peace of mind. Feel the pleasure of victory. Go through this many times. Our physiology and actions strongly influence our inner world. Next time you find the situation arising, take a deep breath and play out your rehearsed response. Put your training into practice. It won't always work; just don't give up trying until you retrain your natural response to the situation. In this way you can change your nature (and it becomes second nature).

You can also use this to develop positive traits. What would a calm, generous, playful person be thinking, saying and doing in this situation? Start to train yourself in these areas. Some people say 'Fake it til you make it.' I say 'Fake it til you awake it.' It's part of you, you just need to learn to bring it out.

Let It Flow and Let It Go.

I like this the best. If you can nail this it would be a game changer. It takes high level mindfulness.

1. Just notice when the impatience, anger, envy or worry start to arise. The earlier you catch it the better (once it boils over it's very hard to manage).

2. There are always three things you can do in this situation;

   a) Just go with it and let it overtake you

   b) Try to fight it (blame yourself, blame someone else, analyse it,

      repress it)

   c) Acknowledge it, experience it, take a deep breath and just let it wash over you. Let it flow and let it go!

As we will see at length later in the book, your thoughts intensify your emotions. Rather than over thinking, the key is to step away from thoughts and just feel the energy of the emotions arising. Don't block it by fighting it or perpetuate it by feeding it with thought. Just breathe deeply through your nose, feel the physical sensation of the emotion and let it wash right over you. Like an aikido practitioner who sees the attacker and gently, from a place of centred balance, just moves out the way. Play around with this. Obviously the less intense the situation the easier it is to do. Practice with small things like banging your knee and then work your way up to those really challenging relationships. You can do it!

The Test:

Imagine you have a terrible day. You wake up late, slip in the shower, spill your tea on yourself, the annoying neighbour annoys you, you miss the bus …and so on. You are cursing and frustrated. Then someone approaches you and offers you your dream job. To get the job though, you have to be calm and centred, show self control, problem solving abilities and general positivity. They are going to observe you for a couple of days to see how you deal with life. The next morning you wake up late and are about to freak out, when you remember you are being tested for suitability for your dream job. You take a deep breath and go to have a shower. You slip in the shower, bang your elbow and are about to scream, when you remember - the job. You stretch it out and let go of your frustration. By the time your tea spills on you, you are just so chilled you make another cup and head for the bus. You wave and smile at the annoying neighbour, miss the bus, so you just decide to walk…. You get the idea. Once we see life with all its challenges as a test to help us grow, it becomes much easier to be the person we want to be.

Play around with these three tools of character refinement. You'll win sometimes; sometimes you'll lose and want to give up. Don't worry - the game of life keeps on going - you'll have another chance to practise.

Complete Well-Being. The 4 Aspects of Your Self.

Along with our character traits and values, there are 3, some say 4, aspects of you.

Physical (Body)

Emotional (Heart)

Mental (Mind)

Spiritual (Soul).

Consciously working on having health, balance, strength and vitality in these areas is a major key to basic well-being, fulfilment and happiness.

Physical (Health)

The healthier you are, the more energy, vitality and resourcefulness you have. You can get up earlier, achieve more, feel more alive and it also helps you deal with the physical and emotional trials and tribulations of life. There are hundreds of great books about building and maintaining physical health. In our spirit of simplicity and practicality, I'm just giving a few key basics that we should all invest in.

In order to stay healthy there are a few simple rules (that you know already).

Rule One: Exercise.

You need to do some exercise. That doesn't mean four hours in the gym a day, but it does mean some sort of prolonged, somewhat strenuous movement of your body. Go for a run or a swim. Play some ball. Do a yoga class. Take the stairs instead of the elevator. It could even be just five minutes of stretching followed by 20 push ups and 20 sit ups. If you incorporate even just that into your daily routine you would definitely reap the benefits. Expending energy actually increases energy and resilience. It's also important as you get older to have good muscle mass to stay strong and mobile.

Be aware of what your body needs during the day. Get up from your desk to stretch and loosen your neck and shoulders / look away from the screen.

Rule Two: Don't put things in your system that are not good for it.

Putting vinegar in a Ferrari is not wise for optimal usage. Smoking, excessive alcohol, fatty foods, sugary foods, gluten, processed food - these things don't lead to a healthy system. Just because something is physically pleasurable (and therefore sometimes in the short term emotionally comforting) doesn't mean it's worth consuming, seeing as there are long term detrimental effects.

Just as important as, or maybe even more important than what you eat is how much you eat. Overeating is incredibly unhealthy and unproductive. It reduces energy and creates several health problems. Filling your stomach beyond capacity means the food can't digest properly (just like clothes in an overstuffed washing machine don't get clean). Make yourself a plate of food that is approximately the size of your stomach. Eat it and then wait 15 minutes to see if you feel full. If not, eat a little more. It's also not advisable to eat for a couple of hours before you sleep. Your body won't get the rest it needs seeing as it will be digesting all night.

Rule Three: Give your body the fuel it needs.

Give your body stuff that gives it energy and strength not things that it has to contend with. There's no one diet for everyone, and I have seen 'authoritative' and completely contradictory research as to the best eating habits. So you should do research, get tested and work out what gives your body health and vitality. A few things that it seem universally agreed upon:[8]

Water is key. Apart from drinking enough water during the day, a large part of your diet should be high water content foods ie salad - cucumbers, lettuce etc. It's better not to drink whilst eating or after for a bit, it dilutes the digestive fluids. Protein is important for muscle growth but too much meat protein can cause health issues. Fruit shouldn't be eaten after a meal seeing as it gets blocked behind other food and can't digest properly and causes gas. Vitamin and mineral supplements help boost the system, get tested to see what you need. It's good to feel hungry for a bit, it helps your body break down waste materials.

Now let's be real. To be practical and sustainable, everything must be in moderation. We're not all meant to be top class athletes. Some people are such health freaks they are actually quite unhealthy. So have some chocolate and snacks, the occasional pint of beer - just realise what effect it has on your system. Once these things start becoming a habit, or you are dependent on them to calm yourself down or deal with emotional issues, or that they are the highlight of your day, that is when it becomes a problem.   Once you see

---

[8] Just waiting for someone to hit me with the latest research to disprove all these things …

that the benefits of being healthy far outweigh the 'benefits' of the unhealthy things you enjoy,[9] you will be able to have more self control (we'll talk more about this later) and invest in the things you need to reach peak performance.

Two other majorly important factors:

Calming the Senses.

We are being bombarded all the time through our five senses. Car horns, people shouting, bad fumes and pollution, news headlines, challenging emails and conversations, stubbing a toe, sports injuries, violent shows, bad tasting food. It doesn't make for a healthy and calm system. This is one reason why many people are highly strung and uptight. It's important for your system to take some time to calm your senses. That could mean listening to gentle, positive, meditative healing music, smelling natural essential oils such as lavender, looking at the blue sky, a

---

[9] I'm sorry to say this (and this is why it's in a small footnote, please don't throw the whole book away just for this), but weed really isn't serving you in the long run. I speak from experience. Yes it can help you relax. Yes you can have some amazing insights about life and deep meaningful conversations. Yes it helps you focus better on the video game and enjoy the movie more. However, in the long run, and between highs, it's taking away from your clarity of thinking, your vitality and consciousness, your emotional and mental health. Look around you - weed smokers are not the most accomplished people you know. It creates a cycle of reliance, a superficial way to deal with life's challenges. I'm not saying to never smoke again. I'm just saying be more conscious and more prepared to put in the effort to tap into higher ways of living without getting high. There are better ways to relax, better ways to deal with your issues, better ways to be present, better ways to tap into spiritual highs and fully enjoy life than sparking up.

flame or a beautiful nature scene, spending time in nature, sucking a piece of chocolate, having a hot bath, turning off the phone data for an hour before bed. Grounding yourself to release built up electromagnetic waves from the internet and phone by walking barefoot on grass is also great for overall health.

These things make you feel well nurtured, calm and resourceful meaning you can deal more easily with life in general.

Breathing.

Breath is quite literally keeping you alive. You take around 23,500 breaths a day. How many of them are deep, slow and conscious? Slow, conscious breathing has immense physical health and vitality benefits. Breathing through your nose rather than your mouth has been proven over and over again throughout time and cultures to be incredibly important when it comes to physical health. Try to at least breathe *in* through your nose as much as you can. Breathing more deeply and consciously also takes you to a deeper and calmer place within yourself. Life can be like treading water with many waves of responsibilities and desires and issues coming towards you. Yet, just like at sea, the waves are only on the surface. Deeper down it's calm and quiet. Connecting to your breath brings you into the present moment and gives you a break from treading water. (See appendix for some simple meditation and mindfulness techniques).

Emotional (Balance)

Some people (I'm a British man, I know this well) are pretty much completely cut off from their emotions. Something happened when they were young, they got teased, had some painful experience and a barrier went up. We don't like to feel emotional discomfort so we repress it. We learn pretty quickly that men don't cry; we drink beer and watch football. This is obviously very unhealthy. The other extreme of emotional imbalance is being totally overwhelmed and controlled by your emotions. You shout when you are angry, overeat when you are hungry, wallow in your misery, make irrational decisions based on emotions, take revenge when you are hurt and can't let any of these feelings go for days on end.

Emotional balance means to be able to experience your emotions fully, without repressing them, but also not drowning in them, perpetuating them or acting on them. It's to be real with how you feel. Self mastery doesn't necessarily mean you'll never feel lonely, upset, frustrated or sad. It's knowing how to deal with those feelings in a healthy way when they arise.

So how do we do this? The highest level would be to let it flow and let it go (see the character traits section). However, very often the emotion is too strong to be able to do that.

So we need to understand the difference between pain and suffering. Pain is an unpleasant feeling. Either physical, when you bang your knee, or emotional, when someone passes away or you split up with your partner. Suffering is a mental process. It's your mind not engaging with the pain in a positive and empowered way. It's the voice that, when you feel lonely, says "Why am I lonely, I'll always be lonely, it's my fault I'm lonely, it's not fair I'm lonely, it's her fault I'm lonely, if I was married I wouldn't be lonely, ..." and so on. These thoughts not only take you away from just experiencing the emotion, they actually build, feed and perpetuate the pain. (remember - If it doesn't work, don't do it). Have you ever felt upset about something and then said to yourself "I shouldn't be upset by this." Well how did that help!? Now you're upset that you're upset! We need to learn to validate our emotions and be able to acknowledge and process them.

One time when my daughter was three years old we were in a restaurant and she went to the bathroom with her older cousin. They came back a few minutes later and my daughter was very upset. I asked her what happened, and she said "I wanted to go first, but she went first!" There was a part of me that wanted to just say "Really!? You're upset about that?! What's wrong with you? That's so insignificant! Look at all the amazing things you have in your life and you're getting upset by silly little things like that?" But, because I read a parenting book I didn't say that. Rather I just said to her "Ow. You're really upset by this aren't you? You really wanted to go first didn't you? I'm sorry. Maybe next time you can go first." Having been heard and validated she completely got over it and went and played. Now obviously, there are much more painful things we go through than what my daughter went through. It's much harder to process incredibly significant and painful things. However, the process is the same. To be able to validate the emotion, to cry if you need to, instead of repressing or expressing it in a harmful way (harmful to yourself or others). Therefore, the key is just to be able to just sit and feel the pain, jealousy, sadness, anger, loneliness, without that voice commenting on it, without fighting or escaping and without reacting to it or making your decisions based on it.

In practice you could just sit with your hand on your heart, breathe deeply and gently say "I feel really sad/angry/lonely now, and that's okay." When the voice of your mind starts chiming in with all its comments, just breathe deeply, catch the mind (don't fight it - we'll see about this in the next section) and return to just feeling the feeling. Be open to crying, screaming (not at anyone else of course. For example when you're in the car getting frustrated at being stuck in a traffic jam). Calming your senses also helps with this. Very often, after five minutes or so, the feeling gets processed and dies down or disappears, *as long as you aren't building and perpetuating it with thoughts.* If it doesn't go and you realise you are just wallowing in negative thoughts, you could feel it for a few more minutes and then get up and do some exercise, painting, music - some healthy creative expression to help you move on until you can find time to try it again. This is the healthy balance; to acknowledge, validate and experience how you feel. Then you can express it in a healthy way; talk to a close friend, journal about it, do art or music (I play the keyboard to myself). The key is to be present with it and feel it, then to let it go or at least, rather than being controlled by it, get up and do what you need to do anyway. I'm not saying it is easy, and real abuse and trauma needs really specific healing methods - body work, somatic experiencing and others. However this is a very useful general idea to help deal with everyday challenging emotions.

Mental (Strength)

This really is the key to everything, as you have probably realised seeing as we keep coming back to it throughout the book. Your whole experience of life is dictated by your thoughts. Positive thoughts lead to positive emotions, negative to negative. Your state of mind creates your experience of life. You may have noticed by now that you are thinking non-stop from the second you wake up until the second you go to sleep. The voice in your head just doesn't shut up all day; hoping, criticising, doubting, judging, comparing, desiring, regretting, planning, appreciating, reminiscing, commenting ... non-stop! Now, what percentage of your thoughts would you say are uplifting and sweet and positive? For many people it's not such a high figure. If you had a friend who spoke to you non-stop like that, you'd probably want to kill them. This shows that we clearly are not in control of our thoughts. Who would choose to have not nice thoughts? In the car, if you don't like the music you change it. You don't just sit there for three hours listening to it. So why do people spend hours obsessively thinking about what people think of them, worrying about exam results, saying negative things to themselves, going over the speech that they want to give to the person who upset them over and over again. Just change the channel!

So what are you going to do? One way is to try to escape from the voice - social media (actually makes the voice worse), netflix, partying, work. That, as I'm sure you know, isn't a real solution. It's a temporary escape. You come home after a hard day at work and veg out to a screen, you haven't actually helped solve the problem. You wake up with the same issues in the morning.

What we need is to develop mental strength. Mental strength is the ability to choose what thoughts we engage in and make significant and which one to let go of. It means to take control of what is going on in your mind rather than being a victim to whatever soundtrack is playing in there. The foundational practice to help with this is some form of meditation. Meditation is defined as the practice of calming and controlling your mind. See the appendix for some basic techniques.

For now, there are other moment to moment mindfulness practices we can employ. Take this analogy. When someone goes surfing, they paddle out and then turn to face the beach, ready to catch a wave. Do they get on every wave that comes along? Absolutely not. Some are too small, some are too big, some are heading straight for the rocks. So what do they do when those waves come along? They don't repress, fight or ignore the waves; you can't do that. What they do is acknowledge the wave and then pull a turtle or duck roll. What this basically means is they are aware of the wave, have judged that it's not beneficial to get on it, so slip under the wave and let it wash over them. You must understand that thoughts are like waves. They come and then naturally move on, unless we jump on them and ride them. All we have to do is be conscious enough to choose which thought waves to ride and make significant, and which ones to let wash over us. As we mentioned before, there are three choices we can make when a thought comes into our mind. We can

a) choose to carry it on (ride the wave),

b) choose to fight it (judge it and ourselves, blame others, wish it wasn't there - jump on other bad waves) or

c) choose to just be conscious enough to identify and acknowledge it and let it flow passed. (let the wave wash over us).

My nine year old son once came up to me with some money he found on the floor which I had dropped. He gave it back to me and then said "Dad. When I first saw the money, my negative voice told me to take it. But I didn't listen to it because it wasn't the right thing to do, so I just gave it back." Incredible. My daughter when she was four said "Dad, my negative voice told me not to share my toys, but I didn't listen to it and I shared them anyway." They identified the voice but didn't listen to it. They also didn't beat themselves up for having a bad thought, or fight the thought, or blame anyone for the thought. They just acknowledged it and didn't engage in it. Unlike emotions which need to be validated and engaged, most thoughts need the opposite; acknowledgement and then complete invalidation.[10]

Now let's be honest; this sounds good, however very few people are on a high enough level of consciousness to just let the negative waves go as they arise. They are already riding that wave towards the rocks before they even notice it. We have ingrained thought patterns and beliefs and just automatically go with them without any awareness. So what do we do at that point? Well, you should know by now! It's exactly the same three things. Once you become aware you are thinking unproductive, negative thoughts you could

  a) Carry on riding that wave … not a good idea, you're going to crash into the rocks

  b) Fight the wave … what's wrong with me for thinking about this again, it's her fault, it's my fault, I hate this

---

[10] Of course, you could misuse this tool to ignore and deny thoughts that you should engage in, which even though they are unpleasant are helping you improve. If they are valid ie true and useful thoughts that can help you grow, then they serve a purpose and are not considered negative even if they are challenging.

wave ... all of those thoughts are just other bad waves that are not serving a purpose.

c) Just notice you are on a bad wave and jump off it.[11]

So now the question is - How do you actually do that? How do you just jump off? It's actually very simple. As soon as you notice that you are on that wave (you are thinking about her again, you are rehearsing the speech you want to give the person who hurt you, you are beating yourself up for something, the voice is saying you don't deserve to get off the wave...) just take a deep breath, stand up a bit straighter, loosen your neck and shoulders, smile and say "I don't need to be on this wave." As soon as you choose to get off and not make it significant, you are off! It's really as simple as that. Yes, you will probably get back on pretty soon afterwards, smash into some rocks and drown in some waves. That's normal. It takes time to retrain yourself and the way you think. However, once in a while you'll catch yourself on a bad wave and just get off. It will feel incredibly exhilarating! You'll realise - I can actually do this! Then you'll get smacked down by some more waves.

---

[11] The same analogy works with buses. Once you realise you are on the wrong bus you can carry on riding it, analyse why you are on it or just get off. When you are more conscious you can just be aware enough to not get on the wrong bus in the first place.

Once you taste victory once, you know it can be done and you'll start getting better at it. It actually becomes a game and as your skills grow you'll start enjoying it more and more.

So how do we know which thoughts to ride and which ones to let go? It's very simple. There is just one criteria. Is this thought serving a purpose or not? Is it helping me grow? Is it helping me feel positive and empowered? Is it changing the situation? Is there something I can learn from it? If it isn't helping in any way, ie it's taking you towards the rocks, there's no point engaging in it.[12] It's as simple as that. As we said (a few times before) we worry about things we can't change, we argue with people we love, we put ourselves down, we get upset when the bus doesn't come or the computer isn't doing what we're telling it to do. Then there are even more painful thoughts which need the same processing. It's a long and tragic story, but I lost my best friend to suicide. He had the biggest heart and smile, touched the lives of thousands of people, but in the end succumbed to his mental struggle. When I found out I had the thought "Maybe I could have done more to help him." A thought like that can destroy a person for life. I sat with my

---

[12] Sometimes a thought can be useful and painful. We can grow from these thoughts too

pain, I grieved, I processed. But I still had this thought to deal with. The first step is to clarify that the thought doesn't serve any positive purpose. For a start, it's probably not true. I was a very good and supportive friend even though we lived in different countries and I called him often. Even if that thought was true, even if there was more I could have done, engaging in it serves no purpose. It doesn't change the situation, bring him back, it doesn't help me grieve, it doesn't empower me or my family who I have to take care of. So when the thought comes, sometimes I feel sad and miss him (see the emotional balance section), sometimes I just let it go and sometimes I use it to motivate me to live a greater life. I don't dwell on all the missed opportunities and all the things we aren't going to be able to do together in the future. Those thoughts don't serve a purpose. I think about the good times we had travelling together. I commit to living a greater life, partly in his honour. In short, I use the memories to create good feelings and I use the pain to create growth and purpose, rather than being a victim to it.

Then, after a while, if the thought isn't being fed and watered, just like a bully who isn't succeeding in upsetting people, it withers away and stops bothering you. I still think about him, and it's still sad, but the thought of "Maybe I could have done more to help him" doesn't bother me so much anymore.

So I'm not saying this is easy. I'm not saying "Chin up lad - just think better."

It takes being real with emotions and feeling pain. It takes becoming more conscious of what's happening in your mind and retraining your thinking. It takes many years of practice. However, it's worth the effort seeing as it's the most important thing you could ever do and the key to living a great and healthy life.

Write a list of negative thoughts and beliefs that often come to your mind and number them. I'm not good enough / I'll never ..../ It's not fair / If only .../ I'm not ...enough.

When you notice them coming into your mind, don't fight them, don't get upset with yourself, don't feed them, just take a deep breath and say "Hey thought number 3, thanks for coming but I'm not riding this wave anymore." Another deep breath. If you are feeling calm, you can then insert a positive opposite thought. "I am good enough." "Everything will be okay" "Okay, I made a mistake - I'll do better next time."

Once you do it once, you'll see that it can be done and with some consciousness and commitment you can completely retrain how you think and therefore how you experience life.

Spiritual Connection

I'm not going to go into this too deeply as the goal of the book is universal wisdom that everyone can agree on, and the belief in a spiritual reality, of Soul and the Divine Creator,[13] is not shared by everyone. However, for those reading this who do believe, it must be mentioned that for a believer everything we said before is true and valuable and can create happiness, self esteem, good relationships, positive impact in the world, a great life; however it is all just a prerequisite for the ultimate goal of life which is experience of and connection to Soul and the Divine Creator of the universe.

For a spiritual person who isn't necessarily religious, the main paths of connecting to Soul and Divine Creator are

a) Meditation: through clearing the mind we can reveal the soul

b) Prayer: the art of forming a relationship with the Divine Creator through authentic conscious conversation from the heart.

c) Purity of thought, speech and action.

---

[13] Some people have an image of Gd as an angry man in the sky with a list of rules and punishments. That's pretty childish. Divine = Infinite (Intelligent, All-Good) Consciousness.

For a religious person, you would also need to be living consciously and joyfully in line with the guidelines of what the Creator wants for and from us.[14]

So there we have it. The more you consciously work on improving character traits and investing in physical, emotional, mental and spiritual well-being and vitality, the more you will experience life on the highest level possible.

---

[14] What exactly that is is beyond the scope of this book. What seems clear though is that an intelligent person doesn't rely on hearsay and faith to form their beliefs. Most religious people are just following the tradition they were brought up with. Intelligent people use reason and logic to do the research and find evidence to demonstrate what it is that the Divine Creator (if one exists at all) wants from us and which, if any, of the books that are claimed to be Divine actually are.

PART THREE:
Improving the World

Going Beyond Yourself

So now we have a clear idea of what it means to improve ourselves. We've learnt some clear steps in order to start doing it and we understand the great benefit of doing so.

However, that's only half the picture.

Sitting in a cave just outside Bodhgaya, the small town that has grown up around the tree where Buddha reached enlightenment, meditating and trying to overcome my ego, a funny thought came to me. Sitting here all day trying to overcome my ego is, well, quite egotistical! Especially when I could be helping in the orphanage in town. It occurred to me that, Yes, personal enlightenment is important, but really what creates a great, extraordinary, meaningful and fulfilling life is going beyond yourself and being there to positively impact the world around you. Most people are thinking about themselves most of the time. What do I want and how can I get it? What do people think of me?

My relationships, dreams, health, problems. Great people understand that it's not all about them; there is a higher ideal.

We're part of a team, part of a movement for something greater. When we think of really great people, we think of the people who positively changed the world in some way.

Now we don't all need to be Martin Luther King. We just need to be people who are there for others, who really care for others, who listen well, who often put others' needs before our own. People who thank the bus driver and smile at the beggar we are giving money to; people who give charity and volunteer our time. We want to be people who others feel comfortable around. We don't want to be roasting, putting down, teasing other people. Happy people don't put other people down; they uplift them. We want to be people who others feel comfortable turning to for support, encouragement and guidance, people who others know are willing to lend a hand, who say kind and encouraging words, people who are looking for opportunities to uplift the lives of those around them, people who, rather than asking 'what's in it for me?' ask 'what can I do for others?' Those are the greatest people, living the most fulfilling lives.

You may be thinking that the whole first half of the book is pointless then! It's so self centred working on myself so much. However, that's a mistake. To work on yourself in order to be able to go beyond yourself is not self centred at all.

A doctor can only help others by helping themself first - getting an education, taking care of themselves - the more you have developed yourself the more you can help others. We want to fill ourselves up so much that we feel we are basically taken care of and then we can overflow and impact those around us.

Identifying Your mission

Beyond just being a nicer, more helpful, giving, kind person (which are character traits you now know how to work on), how do you identify what your particular mission in the world is? What project could you get involved in? What real impact could you have?

The first thing is to identify an issue you see in the world that bothers you.

This shouldn't be hard; sadly there are so many terrible issues in the world - starving children, alcoholism, bullying, political corruption, destruction of the environment - the list goes on (and on and on). Now, you may be particularly drawn to one of these issues for whatever reason, but in general there are two indicators as to which areas you can relate to; your privilege and your own pain.

Privilege

I had a wonderful childhood. My parents were loving and supportive, gave me a good education, sport and music, we went travelling during vacation time, basically I had everything I needed. On arrival in Sri Lanka and seeing so many poor kids and orphans I felt a huge responsibility to share my privilege with them. Realising how much I had, I realised how much I had to give. I felt a calling to do what I could to give them a better childhood. So I ended up working in orphanages in Sri Lanka, India and Thailand. I started investing time, effort and money in empowering the people I felt a responsibility towards and eventually did a forty day, 1100 km fundraising walk across the whole of Israel to raise money for orphanages. Many people feel guilty that they had a privileged upbringing. Why did I deserve that when others are suffering? Really though, guilt is not the appropriate emotion. Guilt means you did something wrong. It's not your fault you were born into a more privileged situation. However, what we should feel is responsibility. I have a responsibility to share and spread the goodness that I received. Identify all the privileges in your life and start thinking about how you could share them with others.

Pain

The other side is your pain. What pain and challenges have you had to endure in your life? Being bullied, abusive parents, alcoholism, divorce, loss of a loved one, loneliness. If you suffered through these things and have come to some healing in your own journey, you are most qualified to reach out and be there for those going through the same thing. You can really relate to them, empathise with them, understand them. You can be there for them and hear them and gently guide them in their own healing journey. Doing this will also empower you and help you find some healing, meaning and purpose in your own pain.

Don't Work a Day in Your Life.

So now we identified your particular area, the question is how can you have a particular impact on these people. What do you have to offer that could keep you passionate about your cause? The answer is

a) What you love doing and are passionate about

b) What you are good at (which are often the same thing - we tend to enjoy things we are good at).

What does this mean? One of the greatest sources of vitality and pleasure is doing some form of healthy, creative self expression. It could be sport, art, music, writing, drama, hiking,

66

sailing, travelling, teaching, to name just a few. If you don't have one of these passions, (many people nowadays grew up looking at screens so never developed a healthy creative outlet), go and explore and try things out to find what you love doing. Now, imagine you could use what you love doing to impact the lives of the particular group of people you are drawn to help.

For example, let's say you were bullied as a kid and you love art. You could become an art therapist. Or you had some form of addiction and you love hiking. You could set up wilderness camps for recovering addicts. You love riding horses and you feel compelled to help children with disabilities get more enjoyment in life, you could provide horse riding opportunities at a summer camp for disabled kids. You get the idea. Use what you love doing to empower the people you feel responsible to help. I used to run ten day trips to Thailand for 20 - 30 year olds looking for meaning in life, in which we meditated in the rain forests, swam in waterfalls and volunteered in orphanages. I got to travel, teach and volunteer, and more importantly empower these more privileged people in society to find a cause they believe in and reach out to make a difference when they returned home.

Ideally you could make a living by using what you love doing to positively impact the world. That means you'd never really work a day in your life. You'd be getting paid to do your mission.[15] If that's not possible, you can still be investing in your mission. You could volunteer time, you could donate to organisations that are combating these challenges, you could educate people about the issue and publicise it. There's always something you can do to be supporting the cause you care about. Your passions will still be a major part of your life as well; healthy, creative self-expression is essential for vitality and well-being.

Healthy, Conscious Relationships

Relationships play a major role in our lives, and therefore have a significant part to play in our happiness and well-being. Struggling in any relationship, parents and kids, siblings, work mates, dating, marriage, is incredibly challenging. Once we can understand the art of conscious relationships it makes life much more manageable and enjoyable.

The first thing we need to do is define a good relationship. Relationship is defined by emotional intimacy - we care about each other, focus on the good in each other and want the best for

---

[15] I'd strongly suggest spending your life doing something you love doing for less money than something you don't enjoy for more money as long as it pays the bills. In fact, the less money you need to lead a materialistic lifestyle, the freer you'll be to follow your dreams.

each other. It involves love, respect and connection. A true friend is someone who genuinely wants the best for you and uplifts you, rather than influencing you in negative ways (even though it may be temporarily enjoyable) or takes advantage of you. There is no perfect relationship so they need to be built and constantly nurtured.

Before we look into the key factors that create good relationships, we have to remember that the pre-requisite for healthy relationships is having a healthy sense of self. Your relationship with your Self is primary. If you don't feel good about yourself, if you don't have self respect, esteem and confidence, relationships become needy and confusing. "Love your neighbour as yourself" means you have to love yourself first.

The Three Foundations of Healthy Relationships.

1. Shared Values (or at least mutual respect).

Why do some people become your close friends whilst others don't so much? What turns a casual fling into a healthy long term relationship?

Of course, it's having things in common. We enjoy each other's company. We enjoy doing the same things. We find the same things interesting to talk about. We may have similar backgrounds or experiences.

When it comes to dating and marriage however, it's a bit deeper than that. It really depends on sharing the same core values and beliefs. If someone is a staunch supporter of one political party (Republican/Democrat, Labour/Conservative) and the other is a die hard member of the other, that relationship probably won't work. (If neither cares that much about politics then it could). If someone is devoutly religious and the other is an ardent atheist - probably not best. If one is a humanitarian and the other is racist ... you get the point.

Emotional intimacy based on shared core values is strong and sustainable. Many relationships don't work because the emotional intimacy was created through physical intimacy. How often do I hear the story "We were attracted to each other, it was fun and felt good, but after a while we realised we were incompatible." What does incompatible mean? Different values. Think about this - Have you ever found someone really attractive and then they said something stupid, mean or racist? You actually start finding them less physically attractive! How about someone who is decently attractive and then you get to know them, their ideas, their kindness and values and you actually start finding them more physically attractive. Emotional intimacy based on shared values, dreams and beliefs creates greater physical intimacy as well.

When it comes to other relationships - parent and child or siblings for example - they don't need to share values as long as they can still love and respect each other and not try to force their values on the other one. That in itself would create a close relationship of mutual respect.

2. Healthy Communication.

My wife and I have been married for fifteen years and we've never had an argument. The key is, we never, ever, ever speak to each other. Ha. No, really - the key is we use a crazy relationship tool called 'Grown up communication.' I know it's a bit out there, but bear with me. An argument is "an exchange of divergent views typically in a heated and angry way." Basically I don't care what you are saying, I'm right, you're wrong and I'm going stuff my opinion down your throat even if it is nasty and hurtful. My wife and I don't do that because we love and respect each other and it doesn't create emotional intimacy, it destroys it.

The first rule in grown up communication, and this goes for all relationships, is never, ever, ever, ever put the other person down. Never say hurtful, nasty, critical, angry things. Never shout (or even raise your voice). Never try to make them feel bad. That damages relationships rather than building them. It means that when you feel really hurt, unheard or angry, it's probably not the best time to communicate. Find space to calm down and then engage in conversation. The baseline for the conversation is that we love and respect each other, we value the relationship and want to return to emotional intimacy. Blame and shame don't do that.[16] Don't make people wrong. Speak about yourself, how you feel, what you need, rather than about them. Don't interrupt whilst someone is talking, try to really hear and feel them. Even if you disagree, try to see where they are coming from. Once everyone feels heard and respected, that usually clears up the issue. If there are still practical things to work through, you can do that in partnership - what needs to happen to make this relationship work? How can we do things differently? When we create a safe space for people to be open and vulnerable, to not be afraid to express their feelings, it creates immense closeness. Good communication is the mortar that sustains relationships, bad communication destroys them.

---

[16] Even when raising kids, in which case you have to teach them right and wrong, blame and shame isn't a healthy way to do it.

3. Responsibilities not Rights.

Imagine two people shared a bank account and they both just kept withdrawing from it with neither of them depositing. Very quickly there would be no bank account left. You get the idea.

The power of selfish taking creates all the human-made pain and abuse in the world. Taking power, taking advantage, taking inconsiderate physical or emotional pleasure, taking money and possessions.

Relationships are there to be invested in, they are bigger than the individuals. Our attitude towards the relationship should not be 'What can I get out of this' but 'What can I put into this, what are my responsibilities, obligations, how can I invest in the other person and our relationship?' If everyone takes care of their responsibilities, everyone will receive their 'rights.' If one is giving and the other is taking advantage, that puts immense strain on the relationship and causes resentment (unless the giver is a completely enlightened individual).

A true relationship is one in which each person respects the other and honestly cares about the needs and feelings of the other. Even a child to a parent, at some point should be asking themselves 'What can I do, how can I contribute, what do my parents need?' Even if it's just behaving a bit better, that's a form of giving and investing in the relationship.

People very often aren't committed to working on relationships. Understand that there are always challenges to overcome, misunderstandings, disagreements, that sometimes even good communication can't clear up. At this point, if both parties are really committed to the relationship they'll find a mentor or therapist to help them through. I tell my students that they shouldn't date someone who isn't prepared to go to therapy, as an individual or couple. Willingness to include a third party where needed shows that they are truly committed to personal and interpersonal growth.

This also means a commitment to always focus on the good in the other person. Marriages often fail because when they are dating they focus on the good and overlook the negatives because there are emotional and physical benefits to relationships. Once they get married and the lust wears off a bit and the communication isn't great they shift their focus from the good to the bad and then they fall out of love. Love is maintained by focusing on and appreciating the good in the other, and communicating in a healthy way about the negatives. Of course you shouldn't be naive. There are some truly toxic relationships and you should know when you need to take a step back and protect yourself.

In summary, real fulfilment, greatness and sense of achievement in life comes from moving beyond yourself and spreading love, light, possibility and positivity to the world around you. Find a cause, invest in it and you'll see you get just as much (or more) out of it as the people you are helping.

PART FOUR:
The Three Key Powers For Success

Now we have our vision and we have the understanding, wisdom, tools and exercises to help us integrate it. The next step is the motivation to get it done.

Here are the three key powers you need to achieve your goals.

Desire / Willpower

No-one ever won an Olympic gold medal unless they really wanted to. I mean REALLY wanted to. No-one ever answered the question "Would you like to win a gold medal in the Olympics Games?" with 'Yeah, I wouldn't mind," and then actually won one. The first key to achieving anything in a real way is to really, really, really want it.[17] Anyone who ever won a gold medal was obsessed with that goal. They couldn't stop thinking about it and they invested immense effort and sacrifice in order to attain it. So we see the two ways you can identify how much you want something are

    a) How much you think about it

---

[17] Obviously it has to be a reasonable goal. No matter how much I want to, there is no way, at this point, that I will be the MVP in the NBA. In general we don't really want things we know there is no chance of attaining.

b) How much effort you invest in it/how much you are willing to sacrifice for it.

This goes for anything. If you really want the girl/guy, you won't stop thinking about them and won't spare any effort or money to impress them. If you really want the job you'll stay up all night studying and even miss the party of the year that everyone else is going to.

So ask yourself the question - How much do I really want to be a great person and live a great life? How much do I really want to grow and contribute?

You can discover the answer to this question by observing how much you think about becoming a better person; what it takes, who you can get guidance from, what books and podcasts could help. How much are you thinking about and planning ways to help others? How much conscious time and effort are you expending on improving yourself and being a positive influence? For most people, although these things may cross their mind once in a while (if they didn't you wouldn't have picked up this book), they aren't at the forefront of their consciousness. Their job, relationships, travel, plans, entertainment take up much more of their mental space. Why is that?

The truth is, we identified this before in the living up to your values / living with meaning sections. Why do you want (and therefore think about so much) everything you want? You believe it will bring you pleasure. That's why you want it.

This is exactly why growth is so challenging. Growth takes effort and pain, which seems like the opposite of pleasure. Why is it hard to quit smoking or get out of bed early to go for a run? You want to do those things, so surely just do them. The answer is that you want to stop smoking but you also want the cigarette. You want to go for a run, but you also want to just press the snooze button and go back to sleep in your warm bed. You want to lose weight, but you also want that cake.

We have a conflict of desires, a higher drive and a lower drive.

One is the drive for instant gratification/pleasure and the other is the drive for greatness.

So why is it that the lower drive very often wins? It's because we are driven by pleasure, and what will give you more pleasure in the moment - to smoke the cigarette or to resist it? To get out of bed in the cold or turn over and go back to sleep? To eat the cake or to hold back? Obviously, in the moment, indulging our senses is much more pleasurable than fighting them, therefore that's what we do. The problem with this is that after the temporary pleasure of the cigarette, cake and snooze button, we don't feel that good any more. We have no self respect, we are less healthy, we feel we let ourselves down. If we took the temporary pain of resisting the cigarette and the cake, or the pain of dragging ourselves out of bed on that cold morning, we'd tap into a much higher level of pleasure. When you get home from that run through the park on a crisp morning you feel pumped and full of vitality and self respect. You then have a healthy smoothie, meditate for ten minutes and have a great start to the day.

We forego the deep, lasting, authentic pleasure of improving ourselves and the world around us for temporary, effortless, intense superficial pleasures.

Really, if we internalised this, we would put in the effort and choose the short term pain and struggle of getting out of bed or resisting the cake for the real long term pleasure of health, growth and self respect. Remember the rule: if you want it enough, you'd be willing to put in the effort. The moment you want to give up smoking more than you want to smoke, the moment you want to lose weight more than you want the cake, the moment you want to go for the run more than you want to stay in bed ie you truly internalise what will give you more pleasure - you will do those things. The moment you internalise the fact that you will undoubtedly get more pleasure from resisting temptation and instant gratification than from feeding it, you will want it enough to put in the effort and make the sacrifice.

All you need then is the next power - Self Control.

Self Control.

Who is in control of how you feel and what you do?

Most people would love to say that they are, but if we look at it realistically that's just not the case. We are controlled by so many things! The weather, sports results, insult and praise from others, our physical desires, our emotions…it's a very long list. Do you shout at people you love when you get angry? Do you eat a whole tub of ice-cream when you are sad? Do you base your decisions on your emotions or on what is rationally the right, good and healthy thing to do?

Self control is the ability to think, say, feel and do what is the right and best thing to do, even when it's hard. It means I use my rational mind to make my decisions; I don't do anything that goes against that, and I do put in the effort to fulfil that. I don't repress emotions, but I run them through my intellect before acting on them.

We noted before why the right thing may be hard to do. One of two reasons:

a) The wrong thing is effortless and feels good in the moment.

b) The right thing takes effort and doesn't necessarily feel good in the moment.

How many times have you said "I really shouldn't do this" and then immediately did it? What was the issue? Lack of self control. How did you feel afterwards? Probably not great.

What about things you say you should do but don't? I should get up earlier, I should call my mother more, I should do more exercise. Okay then - if you should, then do! Imagine how you'd feel if you did those things.

One of the keys to personal mastery is the ability to be okay with feeling uncomfortable. Growth comes through challenge and pain. If you always choose the easy, comfortable way because you are afraid to experience discomfort, you will never grow and live an extraordinary life. If you do bicep curls with a pencil it may feel okay, but you are not building muscle. Of course, you have to know your limit. There's no point trying to bench press 250 kilos the first time you go to the gym. We need to take small steps to start training ourselves to feel okay with discomfort and then enjoy the growth that comes from that.

You can start to train your self control in small ways.

a) Contemplation. Before speaking or doing something, ask yourself Is the the right thing to do now? What will the consequences be if I do it? How will I feel afterwards? Just taking that time weakens the pull of the temptation and gives you the space to make the right decision. Be proactive, don't react.

b) Remove yourself from the situation. If you want to give up smoking but everyone around you is smoking, probably better to get some distance from those people. Don't have cigarettes readily available. Don't go to the bar if you are dealing with alcohol issues. Faced with a chocolate brownie that is calling you - literally run away.

c) Replacement. Choose a healthy alternative to do when faced with temptation. Every time you want a cigarette, do 10 push ups. Sometimes when you are about to say something not nice, say something nice instead.

d) Take on some small battles. One time when you reach for your phone to check, just withdraw your hand and take a deep breath instead. One time, when you are about to shout, hold yourself back. Once a week don't have a second helping of food - you don't need it. Have a cold shower in the morning. Get out of bed early to go for a run. Don't go for your first choice dish in a restaurant.

In these small ways you start building your self control muscles so you can use them when you really need them. The key is to clarify the right, best, healthiest decision and just do it no matter what. Then take some time to bask in the glory of growth, self respect and a more positive outlook on life.

Positive Attitude

How is it that some people have everything but are still miserable, whereas others have very little and are perfectly happy?

Many people think that happiness is the feeling I get when things go my way. When my team wins I feel happy, when my kids are doing well in school I feel happy, when it's sunny I feel happy, when people praise me or like my social media post I feel happy. When the opposite happens I don't feel happy. Clearly this is a major mistake. Those things don't create sustainable, authentic happiness. This should be obvious. Firstly, things can't always go your way, and secondly even if you get what you want it may make you feel good for a little while and give you some pleasure, but they won't make you a happy person. Getting the car of dreams isn't going to transform your experience of life. So, people spend their whole life trying to manipulate the external world to always match their desires and not trigger their pain. That's impossible and far from creating happiness it creates frustration and anxiety. Getting everything you want clearly isn't the key to happiness. In fact the opposite is true. The less you want and need, the happier you'll be. You won't be chasing things and you won't be a slave to having things go your way. I was sitting on a hilltop across the lake from Pokhara in the foothills of the Annapurna Mountain Range in Nepal. I used to go there to meditate each morning as the sun was rising over the Himalayas. I suddenly had a moment of inspiration. I realised that all I need to be happy and have a full life was a) meditation (your thoughts dictate your experience of life) b) wisdom from books (so I could keep getting insights and growing c) exercise (to stay strong and healthy). Then I realised - I'll always have those things (even if I am in solitary confinement I'd have at least two of them). It was an enlightening experience, a moment of salvation. I realised I'd be happy for the rest of my life. If your happiness depends on the external world, it isn't reliable and isn't true happiness. This is because happiness is not a temporary feeling based on things going your way. It's a state of mind, a perspective on life.

So we see that there is one thing that if you have it you will be happy no matter how challenging your circumstances, and if you don't, you won't be happy no matter how privileged you are. So what is it? What is the secret to unconditional and sustainable happiness?

Positive Attitude. That's it. If you have a positive attitude to life you'll be happy. If you don't, you won't. Happiness is the consistent state of uplifted contentment you get from having a *positive attitude* to life. Your attitude/perspective creates your reality. If you have a positive attitude to life, the external world is almost totally insignificant. You could be facing challenges and pain, and still experience overall uplifting contentment if you can get a healthy perspective on it.

Defining Positive Attitude - The 6 Attitude Shifts:

What does it mean to have a positive attitude to life?

It means to ..

Focus On The Good and Grow From The Bad/Challenges.

What you focus on becomes your experience of life. If you focus on everything you don't have, or everything that is wrong with you and the world, or everything that could go wrong, you will not be experiencing joyful states of being. If on the other hand you do the opposite and always try to find what is good, in yourself, other people and your situation (without being naive), that will determine the quality of your life. You get good at what you train yourself in. If you train yourself to always look for the good in yourself, others and the world around you, you will start experiencing more goodness in your life. If you always tend towards the negative that's what your experience will be.

I used to run trips to Peru, Nicaragua, Thailand, India and Sri Lanka. They were ten days of hiking, volunteering, adventure sports, meditating in nature, discussing life goals and values. They were truly incredible trips. However, as to be expected, sometimes things didn't go to plan. The bus didn't come, it was raining, the activities were closed. Sitting in a hut by the side of the road, not enough food, pouring rain, one could get depressed. Yet I always saw it as an opportunity to find the good in the situation. The rain in Thailand is warm and refreshing. Rather than being a victim to the situation and feeling as though the trip was being ruined, I'd say "Hey guys - we're in Thailand instead of the office, let's take our shoes off and dance in the rain." We'd take our shoes off, put on loud music and have a dance party, splashing in the rain. That was always the highlight of the trip. Then some days everything was going right, nice weather, good food, beautiful nature; but someone would complain about the cockroach in their room. What you focus on becomes your reality. Train yourself to focus on the good, to do whatever it takes to find it somehow. An optimist is someone who says "I'm sure it will be okay." If it turns out not okay they say "Well it could have been worse," or "I'm sure it will be better next time." A pessimist says "I'm sure it will go wrong," and when it doesn't they say "but it could have been better" or "it will go wrong next time."

Your attitude not only controls your experience of reality, it can also affect what happens to you. Very often your negative attitude can actually make things go wrong. If you feel bad about yourself you'll have unhealthy relationships, if you have a fear of hiking you're more likely to stumble. If you are confident about passing the exam (and/or being able to try again if you don't pass) you're more likely to do well.

The second half of having a positive attitude is growing from the bad.

There's something called toxic positivity which means you try to convince yourself that everything is fine and good. This is obviously unhealthy. We aren't trying to ignore or suppress our emotions. We have real challenges and pain in life. A happy person isn't someone who never feels sad. They are someone who knows how to process sadness in a healthy way and return to their default feeling of uplifted contentment. True positive attitude includes the acknowledgement that some things are painful, and it is not just okay but encouraged and healthy to experience and express the pain in a conscious way. However, we don't become passive victims to the pain, we don't define ourselves by our pain, we don't let the pain run our lives. Rather we look for ways to heal, grow and even use our pain to help others who are experiencing their own pain.

So we have a definition of positive attitude; focus on the good, grow from the bad. Now ask yourself "How positive is my attitude to life?

What percentage of my thoughts are uplifting, kind, non-judgemental and positive? Do I look on the bright side of life or tend to focus more on the difficulties?"

For most people, through no fault of their own (life is very challenging) the percentage isn't so high. So where does our attitude to life come from? How does it develop? The answer, as usual, is nature, nurture and significant events that you go through. Some people are born more chilled out, some more prone to worry. Some have abusive upbringings, some are spoiled, some have wonderful childhoods. Some go through traumatic experiences. Based on these things we develop a certain perspective and outlook on life. So now what? Are we stuck with that forever? Are we defined and dictated by our nature, nurture and significant events? Are we a passive victim to these factors? Or could we say "Forget my nature and my nurture; I'm going to work on healing from my pain and developing a positive outlook on life despite my challenges."

I think you know the answer already. At some point we can take responsibility for developing a more healthy and uplifting perspective, despite, and even because of, our challenges.

I'm certainly not flippantly saying this is an easy thing to do. We are not saying 'Cheer up lad, just get on with it.' People have serious issues, pain, abuse and challenges to overcome. It could take years of therapy, healing, coaching, meditation, medication ….It could take immense effort.

Yet the first step is always to take responsibility for trying our best to gently and lovingly, with self compassion, shift our attitude towards ourselves, others and the world around us. The alternative is just being a victim (maybe completely justified), but that will never lead to a healthy, conscious, joyful life.

Before we discuss the practical ways to shift your attitude and develop positivity, (which you know already) let's take a look at the six main attitude shifts we can make in order to completely transform our lives for the better.

Shift One: Healthy Sense of Self

Many, many people struggle with feeling good about themselves. Maybe it is because of something someone said to them when they were young 'You're such a bad little girl!" or "you'll never make it." Maybe it's because their Mum was late to pick them up, maybe they were dumped by their boyfriend or girlfriend, maybe they are comparing themselves to others; it doesn't matter what the case, the underlying cause is always the same; people get their sense of self based on what other people think of them, very often based on superficial values. How we feel about ourselves is in fact the most important factor in how we experience life. If we feel good about ourselves we can deal with the challenges of life much more resourcefully. We are less easily upset and offended. We don't do things we're not comfortable with just to get people to like us. We are no longer slaves to what people think of us. It's incredibly freeing. When we don't feel good about ourselves the opposite is true. We feel down, are easily upset and do things we are uncomfortable with just so others think we are cool.

You can imagine the scenario, probably because you've been in a similar one yourself. Everyone has gone out for a drink. One guy feels he's had enough. He's not feeling great anyway and really doesn't want another drink. Then it starts ... "chug, chug,

chug …" the peer pressure is on. This poor kid has no sense of self. He just wants to look good and fit in. Then someone leans over to him and says "If you don't drink that you're a loser!"[18] The girls are watching so he drinks. He throws up... Everyone cheers. Does that guy go home with any self respect? Absolutely not. He feels awful. He's lying there wondering what everyone thinks of him. I'll tell you an incredibly freeing secret. *No-one is ever thinking about you for more than half a minute.* They're all too caught up in thinking about themselves and what people think of them. You know this because you can check in with yourself. How much do you really think about other people? Very little. By the way, usually no-one else really wants that extra shot of vodka either, they're just doing it to impress others too.

Do you understand that? Girls let guys touch them in ways they aren't comfortable with because what will they say about them to their friends. If she lets him touch her too much she's called one name, not enough she is called another. This is so painful. We need self respect and self esteem to be able to have boundaries, feel good and enjoy life free of the anxiety of needing recognition from others.

---

[18] In fact, it's exactly the opposite.. If you do something you don't want to do, that you know isn't healthy, isn't in line with your values just because of what other people with bad values think of you, *then* you're a 'loser!'

So how do we do that? It's actually very simple. If an unhealthy sense of self comes from external recognition based on superficial values, a healthy sense of self comes from internal recognition based on good values. Let's break it down more.

There are actually three levels: self love, self esteem and self respect.

Self Love

What do my kids need to do to deserve my love? That's right, nothing. It would be awful if they grew up thinking they need to perform in some way in order to receive my love. What could they do to lose my love? You got it, nothing. They can be in big trouble, but no matter what happens, I'll never stop loving them. Everyone is naturally worthy and deserving of love. It's intrinsic and unconditional.[19]

So we know that all things being equal, every decent human being is lovable and worthy. It's just that we don't feel it. We've always had to perform to be loved and feel lovable and people have said hurtful things which we take to heart. So how do we get what we know to be true into our heart? Reason doesn't work with the heart. The heart is not rational, it's emotional. The

---

[19] I think that a really evil person could lose their worthiness and right to be loved, however even in that case they are probably evil because they were broken and abused as a kid, so even they could deserve some degree of compassion and love.

key is what lies between our head and our heart; our mouth. How we speak to ourselves will determine how we feel about ourselves. What messages are we providing for our internal system? "I'm not good enough, I'm such an idiot, why did I do that? What do they think of me? I'll never be able to do that. I always mess up." All these harmful messages are destroying us. If you had a friend who spoke to you like that, how long would you let them be your friend? You'd punch them in the face after one minute. "Why are you being so critical and negative!" All we have to do is change the soundtrack in our mind. Remember, if you are on a long car journey and you don't like the music, change the channel. Start feeding yourself positivity, speak to yourself like you'd want someone to speak to your beloved child.

"I'm intrinsically loveable and worthy. I'm doing okay. I'm going to beat this." When the negative critical voice kicks in again, don't fight it or give it the mic, just acknowledge it, breathe deeply and say "Thank you for coming, but I've got a new soundtrack now."

Don't delude yourself with over exaggerations "I really am the greatest. I'm perfect." Just gentle, compassionate, true, general positive statements.

It's important to note that the voice in your head comes from the messages you were fed as a kid, mainly by your parents. My four year old dropped a vase and it smashed. I'd imagine some parents would scream "What have you done! You're such a bad boy. You're so clumsy! What are we going to do with you?!" With that messaging that kid is going to be in therapy for the rest of his life. My son looked at me in a bit of shock and I smiled and said "It's okay. It was an accident. Everyone makes mistakes. You're such a good boy. Just try to be a bit more careful next time. Move out the way and I'll clear it up." With healthy messaging like this, this kid is going to grow up with a healthy sense of self, knowing that accidents happen and that he should be more careful.[20] If you weren't given that, it's time for you to start being that loving parental voice in your own head.

How you speak to yourself is the most important thing in your life. It determines how you speak to others, how you respond to challenges, how you view the world. It's time to switch channels.

Choose a positive phrase and repeat it to yourself often during the day. If your negative critical voice chimes in, just breathe,

---

[20] There obviously also needs to be some healthy, firm yet non-violent discipline in raising children so the child doesn't get spoiled and they know there are boundaries. In this case however it was an accident and age-appropriate behaviour that didn't deserve discipline.

smile and say "Thanks for coming. I've got a new soundtrack now."

Self Esteem

So self love is free and unconditional. What about feeling good about yourself? Where should self esteem come from?

The key to self esteem is having the perfect outfit for every occasion.

Ok, that was a joke. It comes from being able to down large amounts of vodka in a very short time and not throw up. Ok. It's all about your car. Alright, enough now, what's the real key to self esteem? .

If healthy self esteem doesn't come from recognition from the external world based on superficial values, then it has to come from self recognition based on real values.

The key to self esteem is focusing on your good character traits, your good values, your meaningful achievements. It's why you admire other people, so it should be why you admire yourself.

What about your negative traits and failures? How can you feel good about yourself when you are so full of these things too? Simple. Become aware of them and start to work on improving them. Rather than beating yourself up for having bad traits, congratulate yourself for being aware of them and working on them.

Many people hate themselves because they focus on and define themselves by their negative traits and overlook their good ones. We're going to do the exact opposite. We are going to celebrate and define ourselves by our good traits and values, and also feel good about ourselves for working on our not so good ones! It's a win win.

Write a list of things you like about yourself (not your hair and clothes). I'm friendly, inquisitive, loyal, generous, disciplined, fun to be around, positive, intelligent. Notice your mind will try to sabotage this. You'll say "I'm a good friend" and your mind will say "Really? What about two weeks ago when you ....." Don't get put off. You are a good friend, just not a perfect one. You don't have to be perfect in that area to write it down.

Write a list of acts or achievements you are proud of in your life. I did the right thing even though it was hard. I sacrificed my pleasure to help someone else. I really worked hard for my exam. Focus on these things and start feeling good about yourself.

Now, write a list of character flaws. I can be lazy. I don't have self control. I'm arrogant. Don't feel bad about yourself for them. Feel good about yourself for being self aware. Choose one of them to start working on and feel good about yourself for trying to improve yourself.

Self Respect

Finally we have self respect. How can you look at yourself in the mirror at the end of the day and respect the image looking back at you? Well, why do you respect other people?

The key to self respect is to live up to your values. To have standards and hold yourself to them. To always do the right thing. We did an exercise before when we identified times when you say to yourself "I really shouldn't do this, say this, watch this, eat this, smoke this" and then do anyway. How can you respect yourself if you keep letting yourself down? We also identified the times you say "I really should get up earlier, call my Mum more often, exercise more" but you don't actually do those things.

It's very hard to have self respect if you don't live up to your standards.

The key to self respect is simple; work on doing what you should do and not doing what you shouldn't do![21] It's that simple. Once you do that, it makes no difference what other people think of you or say to you, because in yourself you know

---

[21] The word should, saying you should do something and not doing it, is actually very disempowering. Either do it or stop saying you should do it.

you are doing the right thing. In fact the difference between self respect and arrogance is exactly that; an arrogant person (although they may seem happy and 'successful') is still getting their sense of self based on what other people think of them. They aren't generally at peace because they are dependent on recognition and can't always get it, and so compare themselves to others, often someone else better looking and richer than them. Seeing as they feel good about themselves in comparison to others they also tend to put other people down to make themselves feel better.

It's very important to remember that people who put others down and are negative and critical are not happy people. Happy people don't put others down. They try to uplift them. Therefore if someone is putting you down, don't take it personally. As they say "Hurt people hurt people." It's not your issue, it's theirs.

In fact, the more intense they are, the less it is about you. Someone who has real, healthy self respect, doesn't rely on external recognition and therefore feels at peace seeing they have no need to chase recognition and prove themselves. They can also admit their mistakes and grow from them and they never put others down, in fact they tend to want to help others feel good too.

If you didn't already

Write a list of three things you shouldn't do (or should do less)

Write a list of three things you should do (or should do more)

Now choose one of these six things and put in some effort to shift in that area. Once you actually feel the benefit of growth and self respect you will be inspired and motivated to keep growing in this area.

Another way to look at this, in line with the mission of this book, is that self worth is based on how successful you are. If you define success as money, talents, materialism and looks, your sense of self will be based on those things. If you define success as living up to the top values, improving yourself and the world, you'll get your sense of self based on those things. One of these paths leads to a guaranteed, healthy self image which is in our control, and the other leads almost certainly to the opposite, either low self esteem or arrogance.

Help from friends.

The truth is, although this is clear, it's hard to really stop caring what others think of you. So a major key is to hang out with the right people! People who truly care about you, share your values, are there to love and support each other; a group of people who would never put each other down. As we said before, a friend is someone who wants the best for you and follows through with supporting you. Stay away from toxic relationships, negative people and groups who complain, gossip, banter and put each other down. Rather have a few real friends than a whole group of negative people. You don't need to worry that you won't be popular, because people who would judge you for trying to be a good person aren't real friends anyway and are not worth 'being popular' with.

Shift Two: Gratitude

How often do you sit back, take a deep breath, and say to yourself "I can't believe I'm one of the most privileged people in the world," accompanied by beautiful waves of gratitude and joy? How often when you sit down to a simple meal do you think how incredible it is that you have food again! When was the last time you truly appreciated having legs that work? How often do you walk around with a spring in your step looking at the beautiful surroundings? Do you get excited when you turn on the tap and water comes out knowing millions of others don't have running water?

For most of us, we are too busy with our responsibilities and achievements, or focusing on what we lack or what others have, that we don't have time and mental space to just focus on all the wonderful things in our lives. We take them for granted, and rather than appreciate them, we are always searching for fulfilment in getting more of something. Happiness can not come from chasing our desires; it comes from acknowledging and enjoying what we have.

In an earlier section I told you about the orphanage in Northern India with kids who had no parents (or alcoholic parents who couldn't take care of them), no electricity, no tap water, one meal a day, polio, one pair of rags each and slept on the floor. I noticed they seemed generally happier than most of my friends back home. Some of the least privileged people on the face of the planet, happier than some of the most privileged ones. What could explain that? What was the one thing they had that we lacked? Gratitude. They were truly grateful for the little they had; the one meal a day, their friends and teachers, the opportunity to learn in school. They were sharing one pencil between five kids so I walked into town and bought them each a pencil. They couldn't believe it! "Really teacher!? For me? My own pencil?!"

My friends and I took everything we had for granted and were always chasing more; more experiences, more material stuff, more pleasure. We rarely ever just appreciate the things in our lives which are so much more than the kids in the orphanage will ever come close to having. Gratitude comes from focusing on all the wonderful things we do have, rather than everything we lack, wish we had and see other people enjoying. What you focus on becomes your reality. Focus on your lackings, you feel down; focus on your opportunities, abilities, health and material comforts you feel full and joyful.

Now I'm certainly not saying that you should 'gratitude' your way out of pain. We're not saying that when you split up with your partner just "Stop focusing on what you lost, look at how many nice clothes you have!" That's ridiculous. We can feel pain. However, as a general outlook on life, choosing to focus on what you do have, training yourself to find what is good about your self, your life, your situation will make you happier. Once you are happier and calmer you can deal with life's challenges and pain in a much healthier way.

Take a few minutes every day to breathe and think of all the good things in your life. You can write a list with subtitles: Health (go through your whole body - eyes, eyelashes - life would be a nightmare without eyelashes .....), Material items - clothes, books, passport, fridge etc, Opportunities, Friends, Good memories - most of us have a pretty long list (at least compared to the orphans I worked with in India).

The more you focus on and appreciate what you have rather than wanting more and what others have, the more peaceful and content you'll be.

Shift Three: Go Beyond Yourself / Be a Giver

We have already spoken a lot about the necessity and power of going beyond yourself in order to be a great person living a great life. Many people are completely self centred and spend their lives trying to fulfil their dreams and desires. Think about what you think about. What percentage of your thoughts are about yourself? Your relationships, your growth, your desires, your career, your entertainment, your needs. This is totally natural. Yet a great person is someone who feels basically taken care of to the extent that they are not so needy and can now focus on expanding themselves and taking responsibility for uplifting those around them. Life is much more fulfilling when you are living for something beyond yourself. I've seen that one of the most effective approaches to managing depression is to find a cause, to go beyond yourself and touch the lives of others. Volunteer in a soup kitchen, go shopping for housebound people, visit hospitals and homes. When we spread light it helps us feel worthy and rediscover our own light.

People have even given up their lives fighting for what they believe in. We need to shift from approaching life with the attitude of 'What's in it for me?' to 'What can I do for others?' (Obviously we need to give to ourselves first, otherwise we'll have nothing to share. Yet once we have the first two shifts, strong healthy sense of self and gratitude, we are in a position to put others before us).

Shift Four:

Optimist not pessimist / Everything's going to be okay.

One of the biggest plagues facing the world these days is anxiety. People are very uneasy and worried about the future and their ability to handle things that are out of their control. They create ever worsening scenarios in their heads and suffer from tension and lack of peace of mind. For many people it is the most distressing and harmful aspect of their life.

So how do we deal with it?

Firstly, we need to get a rational understanding, which is the easy part. Then we need to actually train our heart to get on board. On a rational level, we have to clarify that worrying falls into the category of things that don't work. If you worry about something and it doesn't happen, you wasted your time worrying, and if it does happen, worrying didn't help (so you wasted your time worrying). Worrying about your exam results doesn't change the results or make you feel good. You may say that worrying does sometimes serve a purpose. "Because I was worried about missing the bus I made sure I got there with plenty of time to spare." "If I didn't worry about my exam I wouldn't work for it." Whilst this is true, there are healthier motivations for these things. You could make sure you arrive at the bus station with plenty of time without worrying, just because that's a sensible thing to do. You'll enjoy the journey much more. You could work for your exam because you are so excited to pass and all the opportunities that will open up for you. You'll be a happier person and probably work more effectively. So we see that in most situations worrying doesn't help, and even in those in which it does help, there are healthier ways to achieve the same results.

The next thing to consider is your life up until this point. Everything you've ever worried about in your life either

a) Didn't happen (the majority).

b) Happened but wasn't as bad as you had feared (most of the rest)

c) Happened, was bad but you dealt with or are dealing with it.[22]

Therefore it's very unlikely that what you are worried about will even happen, and it's very unlikely that even if it does happen it won't be able to handle it. In fact, the less you worry about it, the more resourceful you'll be to deal with it if it does happen. Therefore there is no need to worry.

Then there's the worst case scenario game. Ask yourself what *realistically* is the worst that could happen. You miss your flight. So you waste money and ruin your holiday. That's bad, but you'd deal with it eventually. You don't get the job. It's very painful and sad, but more likely than not you'll get over it and find something else. Knowing that you can deal with the worst case scenario, and knowing that the worst case scenario rarely happens does wonders for taking the edge off the worry.[23]

I was invited to speak in a large conference for women who were leaders in their community. The goal was to empower them to do more good work, engage volunteers, recruit for trips and take their branch of the organisation to the next level. Two

---

[22] I am very aware that there are some things that people go through that are deeply traumatic and need real specialist treatment - body work, somatic experiencing, EMDR. Even they, with the right support, attitude, time and healing can be worked through. If you are going through something like this I'd strongly advise reading Waking The Tiger by Peter Levine. This section though is speaking to the majority of worries for the majority of people.
[23] For people with serious anxiety this is probably not the best technique to use!

weeks before the conference I was trying to prepare my sessions and realised that business and entrepreneurship really isn't my strong area. I can get away with it, but really my optimal areas are personal growth and empowerment, spirituality and meditation. These were high powered people who needed more than someone just getting away with it. So I played the worst case scenario game. They'd introduce me and I'd come on stage. At that point I'd get stage fright, forget what I was going to say and run off stage. I'd be very very embarrassed and I'd damage my reputation as a great speaker. Could I handle that? Well, I'd go home to my loving wife and children who would love and support me. I'd go back to my amazing work surrounded by great colleagues and students. I'd probably end up giving a TED Talk "How to create greatness through your most embarrassing moment." In short, it would be terribly embarrassing but I'd deal with it. Once I knew I could deal with the worst case scenario, and it was completely unlikely to happen, I chilled out a lot and everything, as expected, turned out great.

Great. That makes sense. We now have a logical grasp of how worrying is unnecessary and doesn't help. However reason and logic don't necessarily help with your heart. You may know that worrying doesn't help, but that doesn't stop you from worrying. Here again we have a simple, yet not easy to master, technique for dealing with future fears. Incredibly, several people I have worked with have said that this simple technique has helped them immensely more than years of therapy. Although this may not cure the cause of anxiety, it helps to manage the symptoms in the moment.

When you are feeling anxious, uneasy, worried, rather than building that feeling by thinking and analysing, just take these three steps.

a) Breathe deeply through your nose and gently stretch and relax your neck and shoulders. Your breath brings you into the present moment more, to a deeper, calmer place within yourself.

b) Find some inner calm through grounding yourself in your body through your senses. For example, smell some calming essential oils - lavender, sandalwood. Put a piece of chocolate on your tongue (don't pound a whole tub of ice-cream). Listen to calming music. Look at the clear blue sky. Feel your body sensations; your feet on the floor, your clothes on your body. Gently rub your heart area. Do these all together.

c) From this calmer place gently say to yourself - "Everything's going to be okay." Whatever your mind and heart start screaming at you "It's not going to be okay, I'll make a fool of myself, it's going to be a nightmare," …. Just breathe deeply and gently repeat "It's okay. Everything's going to be okay." You don't need to repress or fight that voice and feeling; you just need to soothe and comfort it.

Now, are you just deluding yourself when you say everything will be okay? Absolutely not! Because, as we established, it IS going to be okay. It's very unlikely to happen and you'll handle it if it does. Once you are in a more calm and positive place, you can look into uprooting the cause of the anxiety.

Shift Five: From Victim to Victor.

We defined positive attitude as 'focus on the good, grow from the bad.' Our first four shifts have been more about focusing on the good. Now for growing from the bad.

Life is very challenging. We have lots of issues, painful moments, things going wrong all the time. So how do we deal with these things? Of course we aren't going to repress or fight them. That doesn't work. Like we said in the emotional balance section we have to be real with and feel our pain. Then we have a choice. We can let the pain define us and dictate our perspective on life, or we can choose to grow through the pain. Sometimes we may not even be able to fully let go of the pain (for example I work with people who have lost children; the pain will be with them forever), however we can learn to feel it and be real with it and then use it as a motivating force to become greater people. In fact many of the greatest people are the ones who overcame adversity and turned it into growth and purpose. They had to develop patience, resilience, forgiveness, mental strength, self control, positivity. They are also the ones who are able to reach out to support others going through similar trials. In this way they turn their pain into purpose.

So, as always, the key to shift from being a victim to a victor is to shift your internal messaging. To go from "Why me?" "It's not fair!" "If only ...." which is incredibly dis-empowering, to (whist not repressing the pain)

"How can I grow from this?" "How can I use this to help others?" "What is the solution?" Perpetuating the victim mentality is not helping you grow, take responsibility, change or feel good. You can build a great and joyful life for yourself not just despite, but often actually because of the challenges you have been through.

Another key factor in this is to never give up on yourself. If something is meaningful and important, always get up and try again. Many people are afraid of failure. It's because they get their sense of self from being successful and failing ruins that. Someone famously said "You miss 100% of the shots you don't take." Obviously it's the right sentiment; if you don't take a shot you'll never succeed. However the truth is that you don't miss any shots you don't take. You need to take a shot to miss it. That's exactly why people are afraid to take shots, because they don't want to miss. They don't want to look bad. They'd rather not try, than try and risk failure. Once you aren't relying on what others think of you, then failing isn't so bad. It doesn't define you. What defines you much more is how much you keep trying and how you deal with failure. Perseverance is a great trait. One of my favourite quotes is 'The master has failed more times than the novice has tried.' Rather try and fail (in which case you didn't fail - you succeeded in trying), than fail to try at all.

The Three Positive Responses to Challenging Situations.

So, we have seen that you are going to face challenging situations; a bad boss or roommate, a health issue, bad weather when you want to go for a hike, a child not doing well in school… the list goes on. When challenging situations arise you can choose one of these three positive responses to a challenging situation.

a) *Change the situation.* If there is a chance you can fix the problem, go for it. Talk to your boss and say it is unacceptable how they are behaving and you want more money; get a tutor for your kids, take steps to heal the health issue.

b) *Leave the situation.* If your boss won't change, the school is just the wrong school, the restaurant doesn't have the food you want - then you may need to remove yourself from the situation. If the sun is too hot for you you can't change that - so get out of the sun.

c) *Accept and adapt. Change yourself.* If you can't change your boss and you can't leave the job, at that point you have to work on building more resilience, patience, appreciation for the good parts of the job and so on. . Obviously without repressing your emotions (see the chapter on emotional balance), you can feel upset, and then use that to grow. This is difficult to do but creates great rewards and is better than the other option, which is to stay and complain and let it destroy your life.

Once again, these options aren't easy, but neither is being a passive victim.

Shift Six: Trust

This final one is not universal but must be mentioned, seeing as for religious / spiritual people it is the ultimate one and the key to true enlightenment. Trust means that I believe everything, no matter how challenging, is meaningful and is what I need in order to reach my ultimate level of spiritual mastery. It has been brought into my life by the Divine Creator in order to challenge me to become enlightened. We said in an earlier chapter that pain is an unpleasant feeling and suffering is your mind struggling with that feeling rather than trying to heal it or just accepting it. How do you stop pain becoming suffering? Find the meaning in the pain. If you understand why you have to go through the pain, you don't suffer. Like child-birth. It's extremely painful (apparently) but it's not suffering. Sometimes you even choose pain - like going to the gym, it's painful but you aren't suffering. Always try to find the meaning, the growth in the pain. What if you can't find the meaning in the pain? A young child suffers and dies of cancer, people become poor and destitute. We can't understand these things or make sense of them. Trust means that even though I can't understand why this is good and I can't find a meaning, I know there is one. While this might seem very naive to non-believers, one who is living with pure trust certainly experiences life on a very high level.

They never get envious because they believe everyone gets what they need. They don't get angry because everything is as it should be. (they take action against injustice if they need to, just without the anger attached). They don't have fear, seeing as everything works out for the best in the end. They can accept seeming injustice in this life seeing as justice will prevail in the end in the next world. They still experience pain and grieve if they lose a loved one, but don't have the suffering (why did this have to happen, it's not fair etc) that usually accompanies the pain. They never say in exasperation "I just don't need this right now!" because they believe if it's happening they do need it right now. They remain calm and peaceful and positive, knowing that everything will work out great, and that even if it is painful, it is not meaningless. It means they aren't just making the most of the challenges in their life, they are embracing them as exactly what they need to become enlightened.[24]

---

[24] How can one develop this trust? One way is to just be brought up with it or come to accept it as an act of blind faith. The other is to look for logical, empirical evidence and reasons to believe in an Infinite, Intelligent, Conscious, All Good, Involved Creator; thereby creating an Evidence-Based Trust. This is an extremely powerful, spiritual yet rational perspective on life.

Implementing the Attitude Shifts

If you got this far, I feel I don't even need to write this section. How do you switch your perspective? Just switch what messages you are feeding yourself. Notice when you are having negative attitude thoughts, take a deep breath and smile (at your victory for noticing) and just switch to a positive attitude thought instead (processing emotions healthily if you need to). Simple. You could turn it into a game - see how many shifts you can have each day.

How about making a chart? Give yourself a check mark, or sticker or treat every time you manage to switch into positivity.

First Practical Steps

Okay so you read the book. Hopefully you made some of the lists. Now we have to start living it. What is the first practical step you can take right now to start implementing the ideas and slowly building the life you want?

Sit up straight, loosen your neck and shoulders. Take some deep breaths.

Then say to yourself:

"I can do this. I can start creating a better life for myself. It's up to me. Just take some small steps in the right direction."

Then choose ONE SMALL THING you should stop doing, or at least do less, and ONE SMALL THING that you should do more. Write them down.

Then you need support and accountability

- Tell a close friend to check in with you and keep you accountable. Even better, get them to take on the challenge with you.

- Make a chart to measure your progress. Write the days of the week on the top and the task on the side. Give yourself a check mark when you do it. If you see it's blank for a few days, put extra effort in.

- You could have rewards and consequences to help motivate you.

For example; Every time you do the positive action, you put a bit of money aside to buy yourself something nice. Every time you fail you give some money to your friend. (Obviously the real motivation is the self respect, growth and better life you have for doing it and the opposite for not. For now though you may need extra incentives).

That's it. It's the beginning of your journey. Small, consistent steps and you'll arrive at your destination.

Final Words - What are you hustling for?

So that's it. Short, simple and sweet. Everything you need to know to create a wonderful life for yourself. It's not easy, but with some commitment and support, everyone can do it. It just takes investing some time and effort. How much? The more the better, but at least as much time as effort as you are investing in entertainment and social media. It means consciously working on physical, emotional, mental and spiritual well-being. It means reading personal growth books, listening to meaningful podcasts, exercising, meditating, planning how to impact the world around you, letting go of negativity and above all being kind to yourself. It takes managing your mind - not letting the negative thoughts run the show. It takes investing in being good and doing good at least as much as you invest in looking good and feeling good.

It's very clear - you get the results you invest in. Make sure you are investing in the things that get you the results you really want. As we said at the beginning - clarify the goal, identify the steps you need to take in order to achieve it, and just do those things.

I'm not going to wish you luck, seeing as luck has little to do with it. It's up to you. I am going to wish you an immensely enjoyable journey. Just start walking the path, small steps in the right direction. You may wake up one day a few years from now and realise you are much closer to living the life you really want and deserve.

To finish as we began - you don't get to choose when and how you are born or when and how you will die, but you can, and must, choose what you do inbetween.

Enjoy the journey!

Appendix:
Meditation and Mindfulness Practices

We've spoken a lot about the need to calm, quieten and control your mind. Peace of mind, inner calm, clarity and self control are major keys for living a healthy and great life. Your internal systems - digestive system, heart beat etc are all unconscious and involuntary. They just happen. Your external movements - walking, eating - are all conscious and voluntary. There are two fundamental things that are unconscious and involuntary, but you can learn to take control of them; your thoughts and your breath. Your breath therefore is the key to calming and controlling your mind.

The most direct way to develop these things is through basic meditation and mindfulness practices. Here are a couple you can play around with. Try to enjoy it, don't be too intense, just relax and have a go. Like anything, it takes time and practice to become good at these things.

Quietening The Mind.

Find a time and place where you won't be disturbed.

Put on some soft music if you like.

Sit up straight (either in a chair or on the floor as long as you are comfortable), close your eyes. Gently stretch and loosen your neck and shoulders. Start breathing gently, slowly and deeply through your nose, fill up your lungs, then gently release your breath through your nose or mouth. Try to get into a rhythm of breathing in and out - focusing all your attention on your breath.

As you release your breath, try to feel tension and stress leaving your body. When you notice that your mind is wondering (which will probably be after less than half a second), smile, catch it and gently bring your attention back to your breath. Repeat for 3 - 5 minutes.

At the beginning, most of the time will be spent noticing that you are not focussing on your breath as your mind just starts wondering automatically. The key is not to get frustrated, rather to just gently return your focus to your breath coming in and going out. Rather than feeling that it's a failure that your mind wandered, you could see it as a victory that you caught it and returned attention to your breath. Then throughout the day, consciously tap into your breath for a few seconds to re-arouse the feeling of calm.

Mantra

Exactly like you did with the first exercise, only this time you can say a word or phrase in your head to help keep you present.

For example

"Breathing in, breathing out."

"Here, now."

"Peaceful, calm."

Observing Thoughts and Emotions.

Get into a breathing rhythm again.

Then, instead of focusing on your breath, try to observe your thoughts passing through your mind. You could imagine your thoughts as clouds floating across your consciousness, or a river flowing passed.

The exercise is to be an observer; to just watch curiously and non-judgmentally at what thoughts are passing through your consciousness. When you lose the detached observer perspective and 'fall in the river' or 'float away with the clouds' just gently bring yourself back into observer space by focusing on a few deep conscious breaths.

Listening

This one is great for when you are on the train or in the park.

Get into your posture, gently close your eyes and start breathing slowly and deeply. Now, focus on the sounds all around you. Just let the sounds come into your consciousness without labelling and judging them (That's a bird, I like that sound, that a car horn it's ruining my meditation).

Just be present to all the sounds. When your mind starts judging and labelling, just smile, sit up a bit straighter and return to focusing on the sounds.

Imagination

Close your eyes and bring up a memory of when you felt calm and happy. Get a really strong image of you being there, the sights, sounds, and try to arouse how you felt at that time.

Presence

Choose a mundane activity, such as washing the dishes, and try to become totally present with it. Feel the warm water on your hands, hear the sounds of the water splashing, the cutlery and crockery hitting together, the sponge squeaking on the plates.

When your mind wanders to the past (good or bad memories, regrets) or the future (plans, worries), just gently come back to being present with what you are doing.

About the Author.

After spending six years living in Asia, delving deeply into Eastern philosophies, partaking in silent meditation retreats, extreme martial arts training, hiking in the Himalayas and a 1200 km pilgrimage around a Japanese island, as well as spending time volunteering in orphanages, Dov Ber moved to Israel and set up a social justice organisation, All for the Kids, which raised money and awareness for orphanages in India, Africa and Israel. He made it into the Israeli Ministry of Foreign Affairs' web-booklet entitled 'Young Leaders of Israel 2010.' He's now a senior Educator at Aish World Centre in Jerusalem, a much sought after motivational speaker, author of 'Mastering Life: A Unique Guidebook to Jewish Enlightenment' and is Founder/Director of Living in Tune: Authentic Jewish Mindfulness which runs on-line mindfulness courses based on Jewish wisdom (not only for Jews - everyone welcome!).

Learn more from him:
www.rabbidovber.org
Online Mindfulness Course: www.litmindfulness.org
Instagram/Tik Tok: RabbiDovBerOfficial
Spotify: Dov Ber Cohen - Living In Tune
Subscribe to his YouTube Channels:
@masteringlifeseries and @livingintune
Be in touch directly: dovbercohen@gmail.com

Made in the USA
Middletown, DE
29 January 2026

27737180R00073